I0540266

COUNTRY FOLKLORE
1920s & 1930s

. . . and that's the way it was

∞

LOUISE K. NELSON

Hope you enjoy the book.

Louise K. Nelson
1997

WORLDCOMM®
a division of Creativity, Inc.

Publisher: Ralph Roberts

Vice President/Publishing: Pat Roberts

Cover Design: **WorldComm**®

Editors: Vivian Terrell, Gayle Graham

Interior Design and Electronic Page Assembly: **WorldComm**®

Copyright ©1997 Louise K. Nelson, all rights reserved.

Reproduction and translation of any part of this work beyond that permitted by Sections 107 and 108 of the United States Copyright Act without the permission of the copyright owner is unlawful.

Printing History:

Printed in the United States of America

10 9 8 7 6 5 4 3 2

ISBN 1-56664-113-6   Library of Congress Number: 96-61902

The author and publisher have made every effort in the preparation of this book to ensure the accuracy of the information. However, the information in this book is sold without warranty, either express or implied. Neither the author nor WorldComm® will be liable for any damages caused or alleged to be caused directly, indirectly, incidentally, or consequentially by the information in this book.

The opinions expressed in this book are solely those of the author and are not necessarily those of WorldComm®.

WorldComm®—a division of Creativity, Inc.— is a full-service publisher located at 65 Macedonia Road, Alexander NC 28701. Phone (704) 252-9515 or (704) 255-8719 fax.

WorldComm® is distributed to the trade by **Alexander Distributing**, 65 Macedonia Road, Alexander NC 28701. Phone (704) 252-9515 or (704) 255-8719 fax. For orders only: 1-800-472-0438. Visa and MasterCard accepted.

This book may also be purchased on the internet in the Publishers CyberMall. Set your browser to http://www.abooks.com and enjoy the many fine values available there.

Contents

Dedicated To:

My children:
Paul and Randy

My grandchildren:
Ken, Laura, and Mary Margaret

In hopes that my children and grandchildren
will pass the memories on to future generations.

...and that's the way it was.

INTRODUCTION

I was inspired to write this book, *Country Folklore...and that's the way it was*, by my family. My mother and my uncle lived until they were in their late 80s and early 90s. My uncle could remember all the ways of country living in the 1920s and 1930s. In reminiscing with them and my family, I tried to capture all these ways of living. I first wrote a book "Country Living With Grandpa" in his own language. My grandparents had no schooling and their language was typical in this era of life. By living with my mother, my siblings, my uncle and my grandparents this book is very real and has touched many people.

My grandparents were very poor tenant farmers, but this didn't hinder them from making a good living. They learned to save, preserve and can fruits and vegetables and to make our clothes from feed and flour sacks. We learned to cope with life by sharing and loving each other, by doing extra work to have the food and clothes we needed and to be happy. I can't say we were unhappy to live in this time of life because we weren't. This is the way all the farmers lived. After the one-room school closed, we went to better schools and became educated. Then we were ready to move on with the changes of the world, but this didn't stop us from the happy memories of living our early lives in the 1920s and 1930s.

So many of you lived this same way and have told me how you enjoyed the writings of early farm life that I've had in the local paper. After countless requests, I have put these in book form so that our grandchildren and great-grandchildren will be able to see just how life was as we grew up.

Louise K. Nelson
51 Asheville Rd.
Waynesville, NC 28786
704-456-3760

MEMORIES OF BIG BRANCH

Big Branch, the setting for the stories in this book is located in Haywood County near Waynesville, North Carolina. It is a unique community with coves, hollows, meadows, hilly land, pastures, ridges, farm land, woody mountains, and a big branch that runs through the entire community. Plus all this, there is a road from the entrance of Crabtree and Hyder Mountain. There were trails from each home leading to every home in the community which were well used. There were trails leading to the community doctor's home and the Crabtree Baptist Church. There were trails leading to the country stores.

The branch begins with streams drifting down the mountain and from the many mountain springs, forming to make a big branch as it traveled through the community and dumped into the Pigeon River that flowed on into Tennessee.

Big Branch community is nestled between coves and mountains. It is a very beautiful community. The community consisted of approximately thirty families.

Most of the families owned their land. My family lived as tenant farmers on about 225 acres owned by the Bill McCrary family.

In saying my family, this was when we moved into the home of my grandparents, Wiley and Dollie Caldwell, after the death of my father, Garrett Kinsland.

All the families including the children were taught to work, to save, and to love their families and their neighbors.

Almost in the middle of Big Branch was a one-room school with seven grades and one teacher. There were twenty-one to twenty-five pupils.

When the school was not in use it was used for community gatherings such as box suppers, church services, etc.

The families in the entire community gathered for corn shuckings and pea shellings, hog killings, molasses making, and Sunday afternoon ball games.

This is where we learned the ways of country living. We were happy and didn't know that the world was different elsewhere.

We got a lot of enjoyment just roaming over the mountains and through the many trails that led to our neighbor's homes.

We all lived the same in the community and we were happy and content to do so.

As I look back over the years, I am so happy that I was able to live and learn as we did in those days.

OUR MOVE TO GRANDMA'S AND GRANDPA'S

I remember the way Grandma and Grandpa's house looked at the time my family moved in with them — early 1930s.

Actually, the house was two houses joined together with a porch on one house and an opening between the two houses.

The kitchen was the oldest house, and it was one big room, made with logs, with mud in between them. It had a handmade shingle roof. There was a big fireplace and a wood cook stove. There was no electricity, no running water; therefore, no sinks for washing dishes and no indoor baths. There were two windows and one door. The windows were wooden shutters. When open, flour sack curtains covered the opening to keep out flies and let in some light. Then at night the wooden shutters were closed. Inside you could climb up a ladder and there was a little space (called the loft) for storage.

There was an eatin' table, a wash table, a long bench behind the eatin' table, and a work table with lots of things sitting on it. The wash table had buckets of water, a dipper, a wash pan with a saucer of soap. On a nail near the wash pan was a towel made from a feed sack.

The children sat behind the table to eat. All of us sat on the bench. There was also a bench the length of the table in front and straight chairs at the ends.

11

Big Branch -1929
Grandma Caldwell, Ruth, Flora C. Kinsland, Mazie, Garrett Kinsland, and Louise Kinsland.

On the eatin' table was an oil cloth covering. There was a sugar bowl and a spoon holder, which was made from a round oatmeal box, cut to fit the spoons.

There were jars of kraut, smoked fruit, a churn, and a jar of cream getting just right to churn. The kitchen cabinets were called "safes." There were lots of straight chairs. On the mantel (fireboard) were medicines and matches and a button box. There was always a basket of fresh eggs and basket of Irish potatoes.

Hanging behind the cook stove were dish cloths, dish pans, pots and pans for cooking. There was a wood box with sticks of stove wood.

That's about the extent of the kitchen.

Now the other house was one big room downstairs and one big room upstairs. This house was made with logs and had a tin roof. There were two doors downstairs with a small opening in the bottom of the door where the small dog and cats went in and out.

Downstairs there was a fireplace with two windows by it. There was an opening under the downstairs. In the winter months pumpkins, candy roasters and apples were kept there. They were kept near the chimney to keep from freezing. In the downstairs room were beds (bedsteads), dressers (bureaus), straight chairs (cheers), and two sewing machines.

Upstairs were beds and beds. We had feather pillows, some feather beds and some straw beds (straw ticks). Covered cans would be sitting around. There were boxes of sweet potatoes rolled in newspapers (to prevent freezing). Wires were strung up to hang clothes, and clothes also were hung on nails. There were a few bureaus and straight chairs. We hung clothes up the stair wall, also.

The walls in all parts of the house were covered with newspapers, and overhead the ceiling was covered with cardboard boxes to help turn cold air out.

Both parts of the house were very cold. The only heat in the main part was a fireplace.

This was not a very good house, but we were thankful to be there. Our father had passed away and left Mother with six children. It looked like the only hope was to send the children to an orphanage, but our grandparents took us in. In addition to the seven of our family, my grandparents

Zimmery Caldwell, Sam Massie, Wiley Caldwell (my grandfather), Mercus Massie, Garrett Kinsland, (my father). Just around the curve to the left was the one room school.

had two children still at home and were keeping two of grandpa's sister's children who had lost their parents. There was wall-to-wall people, thirteen in all.

We survived the hardships and our family stayed together. We learned to cope and found ways to make ends meet and were thankful to our grandparents and to God for providing us with a way to stay together.

My grandparents were tenant farmers. Their only means of making money was a tobacco patch and what eggs and country hams they could sell. They preserved everything they grew. There was always plenty of food, even though my grandparents were very poor.

In spite of the crowded conditions, the house was kept quite clean. We were devoted to each other because of these hardships.

A cellar

A corn crib

THE FARMHOUSE BUILDINGS

When we moved into the home of my grandparents in the early 1930s, there was a group of buildings around the farm. We couldn't understand so many buildings.

"What are all these buildings for?" we asked Grandpa.

"Well," replied Grandpa, "this is the *cellar*. Grandma and your mother will store all their filled cans here. Part of the building is in the bank and this keeps the cans from freezing.

"Now this building is the *chicken house*. The chickens roost on those poles at nighttime and they lay their eggs in the boxes.

"This building with the slats and open section between is the *corn crib*. That's where we store our shucked corn. Every Friday night we shell corn, and I take it the mill on Saturday to grind into meal for mush and cornbread. We also feed it to the hogs.

The chicken house.

15

The hog pen.

"This pen is the *hog pen*. They stay here and in the lot until time to kill them, so we can make sausage, ham and lard.

"The building here is the *smokehouse*. After the hogs are killed and cut into the right pieces, like ham, middling meat, and fat back, we store it here in the shelves and hang the hams in flour sacks to cure.

"This little building is called a *duck coop*. This is made for the ducks to sleep in. However, they don't always. They sometimes sleep right here on the bank. They lay their eggs in the morning up and down the branch bank.

"Right here at the spring is the *springhouse*. You see the water runs all the time from the spring into the springhouse and in the troughs and we store our milk and buttermilk in buckets. Butter and other foods we have left over are stored in buckets and pans. All these clean rocks are placed on top of the pans to keep them secured in the water.

"Now, let's go out to the *barn*. I want to show you what all the barn is used for.

"The sheds on the side here are used for storing farm tools and equipment. The other side of the barn is cow sheds. The milking cows and baby calves are in the sheds and the horse stays in this one. In the fall of the year the tobacco is hung in the main section and in the hayloft to cure.

"After we work up the tobacco and sell it, the cattle come

Tobacco curing

in out of the cold in the winter months. The hens love to come up here and make their nest and lay their eggs. I usually find a basket full when I'm getting hay down for the cattle.

"The sheep hardly ever come in the barn, but when we shear them, they are brought down in the fenced area and we shear the wool off. Grandma uses the wool for making quilts.

"You know what this little building is? It's the *doghouse*. He stays here close to the house at night time. If anyone come close he barks.

"Then there is this building over the hill. This is the *outhouse (toilet)*. Inside the toilet is always an out-dated Sears, Roebuck catalog.

"This is the *woodshed*. It is nearly always full of stacked

wood, especially in the winter months. We chop wood outside here on the chop block. The chop block is a huge block from a tree. The ax stays in the chop block or will be hanging along with the other tools and the tubs used for washing on the springhouse.

An outhouse

17

The still standing homeplace of cousin, Willie Kinsland.

"This is the sawhorse. Two of us pull the crosscut saw through the logs until we saw the wood in pieces, and then we chop it in sticks.

"Down below the house, close to where we have the cane patch, is the *molasses shed*. The molasses mill is kept covered over until time to make the molasses. On the wall are dippers and stirrers and other things we use when making molasses. In the fall of the year just before frost, we cut the cane, pull off the fodder, and stack the cane away from the frost until there's time to make the molasses."

"Well Grandpa, it sure takes a lot of buildings for storage and for animals. We're going to have fun here on the farm," we said.

We did have fun living with grandma and grandpa and helping feed the animals and canning for the cellar and carrying water from the spring.

I still have pleasant memories of all the things that had to be done on the farm to survive. What a wonderful place it was.

All the old buildings that remain standing are about to fall down. I just ride in the country where I grew up and take pictures of these old buildings and reminisce about these days gone by.

THE FARM ANIMALS

I lived back in the days when an animal around the farm or the house had its reason for being there. We became very attached to the animals. Every animal had its place and was very useful.

The cow provided milk, butter, and meat for the family. Cattle were sold and money was used to pay expenses on the farm. Sometimes, there were too many baby calves, and at a certain age they, too, were sold.

The horses were used to help with the work; like hauling loads on the sleds or wagons, pulling logs for wood, plowing, etc. They were used in the older days for pulling the buggy. They were also used as pleasure horses for riding.

The chickens were a must. They provided eggs and meat for the table as fried chicken and chicken with dumplings. The rooster was the alarm clock for the country. When ours started crowing before daylight to tell us it was time to get up, the neighbors roosters were also crowing. Seems they tried to outdo each other.

The ducks provided eggs and meat. They were useful also for feathers for a feather bed or pillows. They were so beautiful swimming in the pond. It was a familiar sound with all of them quacking.

The guineas were a good source for eggs. However,

A flock of guineas and a pigeon.

their eggs were small and their nests were very hard to find. They didn't want a nest near the house. Lots of them laid in the same nest. Not many farmers kept guineas.

The hogs were the main source of meat for the farmer's table. They did no work. They just waited to be fed. At meal time they squealed until their food was brought to them.

Turkeys were used for meat. When company arrived they were baked and went a long way to provide meat for a crowd. It was another familiar sound to hear dozens of them gobbling at the same time.

The cats were used around the house and barns to keep the mice killed. There was nearly always a house cat and a special pet for a child.

The dogs were used for hunting. They used them to rabbit hunt and the rabbit was used for food. The hunters used them to kill animals so they could sell the hides to make money. They were helpful in herding cattle. They always warned you when someone approached the house, and sometimes they were the source of letting you know that someone was around that didn't need to be there.

The sheep were used for meat, but their main purpose was to provide wool for clothes and quilts. The farmers had lots of sheep and they sheared the wool for selling, also.

A goat

The goats were used only for clearing the spots of land that were in bad need of clearing.

One of the neighbors had donkeys and you could hear them braying from their farm.

My grandfather and the landlord had mules for working. You've heard the old saying, "Stubborn as a mule." Grandpa's mule was very stubborn—so stubborn that he would say, "Heck." Therefore, the mule's name became "Heck."

The farmer could not get along without all the animals. They were useful. If you could go back to an old-timey farm and see and hear all these animals again, it would be great. The farmer's animals are very few now. Some specialize in just one, not all the animals. There are cattle farms, goat farms, pig farms, chicken farms, and others. No one's farm has all the animals around that they did in the olden days.

I can just see my grandfather's, his landlord's, and every neighbor's farm with all these beautiful animals and hear all the familiar sounds of the country.

MY UNFORGETTABLE MEMORIES

My memories of the Big Branch one-room school are many. I didn't know Mrs. Mildred Wulff, but I know and dearly love Mrs. Bessie McClure Evans (Miss Bessie). My sisters and I visit with them often.

Both teachers have given me permission to use their stories about the school.

Besides all the good teaching that I received from Miss Bessie, I remember what a special person she was and is.

Miss Bessie not only taught us book learning, she taught us some Bible each day. She taught us to love and obey. She encouraged my sisters, Ruth Kinsland and Ruby Sanford, in reading by buying them each a dress. Her thoughts were with the community folks. She bought Jack Caldwell a pair of overalls. She brought treats to us for recess. One special treat was bananas. One boy, Paul Sanford, wasn't familiar with bananas. He first thought is was an overripe cucumber and he tossed it against the school building.

Miss Bessie brought beef stew to the school. The parents furnished potatoes, carrots, and onions, and Miss Bessie cooked a big pot on the top of the pot bellied stove. Sometimes it would be vegetable soup or dried beans. By the time we all smelled this good food cooking, we would all be very hungry.

She arranged to have the Massies' mother, Rena, to cook

Mrs. Bessie McClure Evans, standing, and Mrs. Mildred Medford Wulff teachers of Big Branch School. This picture was taken in 1985.

and carry the hot food to the school room. Mrs. Massie's husband, Mercus, made her a wagon to pull the food to the school.

Other times we would carry our dinner, which would consist of a lot of milk with cornbread crumbled into it. We would place these pint jars in the edge of the big branch to keep cool.

We had fun with the spelling bees, the Halloween parties, the Christmas tree and exchanging presents, the Christmas play, Easter egg hunts, and the trip to Chambers Mountain.

To get to Chambers Mountain, we went by Mericus and Jerry Massie's homes to the mountain where we could see Waynesville, Lake Junaluska, and Clyde.

One particular Easter I remember a contest. The pupil who could get the most words out of "Easter Sunday" would win an Easter basket. The school had one dictionary. We had no dictionary at home, so I borrowed the school's. I spent the weekend looking at each word in the dictionary to see if it was a suitable word. I had many and I won the Easter basket. I never would have been able to do this without the use of the dictionary.

Sometimes we took the long walk to the Crabtree school to visit. I won the racing game with my group.

One of my most memorable things was that Charlie Massie and I were the only pupils in our class and many times we played together at recess. We played a lot of marbles. We also shared a double desk.

We hated for the school to close in 1937 because we were all used to each other and everyone got along so good.

Uncle Jerry Massie came to our school often at recess time. He would throw silver bells and peppermint candy in the grass for us.

A group of Big Branch School students. The year was possibly 1930. The teacher, Miss Bessie McClure, is in the middle of the back row.

GOOD OLD ONE-ROOM SCHOOL DAYS.......

"In the early 20s and 30s I was fortunate to be the teacher at Big Branch School. It was a little frightening to know I was going to be the one teacher for seven grades, pupils ranging from six to sixteen years of age.

The school house was a small, brown, wooden building near a country road with a large branch beyond the road. A beautiful stream, I might add.

The furniture was a one-drawer teacher's desk, a straight chair, chalk board, double desks for pupils with a few single desks. There were three or four windows on both sides. The only door was in the middle of the building on the northern side. The heat for the building was a pot belly stove in the middle of the room.

On the outside, the playground had not been mowed lately. There were two outhouses on a little hill and a pump. Behind the building, as you approached, was the winter coal piled near and partially under the house.

I was told over and over to make lesson plans for each day and each subject. My job was to plan how I could combine grades in some subjects and find time for each class. Also, I had to find time for those who were just beginning.

Our first combined project was health, which some books listed as sanitation. We began by studying about food, balanced diet, and many other subjects.

After a while in school, days began getting cold, and we had to have a fire. We decided to cook one hot dish to supplement our lunch.

In the clear stream, we could place our jars of milk. When it was hot, the milk would not spoil; and when it was cold, it would not freeze. That was our refrigerator. Each student brought their bread, dish, and spoon.

I would cook with the help of the sixth and seventh grade girls. Our hot dishes started with potatoes, beans, and stews of various kinds. As we went along, many of the parents would send food to be cooked.

The second year, the mothers canned many cans of food for school use. A parent let us use half of his garden for corn to take to the mill for corn bread. Bread from the store was almost unheard of.

The W.P.A. had begun to give food to the schools that had lunch rooms. We had no such place, but we had a lovely lady, the mother of the Massie children, who was an excellent cook. She willingly prepared our lunch for the next year.

Each morning we had a short devotion, Bible study, and prayer.

Each class had their turn with the teacher, but there had to be many combinations, such as history, geography, and health. There was a spirit of helpfulness. Each pupil was allowed to study on his own grade level.

Every Friday, the last hour was devoted to entertainment time. Each child was encouraged, not forced, to perform. The whole teaching and learning process was a team effort. Older ones helped the younger ones. I walked to school from Hyder Mountain daily, morning and night. I guess it was about four miles. On cold mornings my breath would be frozen on my coat, but I kept warm walking.

I went directly through the yard of Aunt Dollie Caldwell, grandmother of the Kinsland girls and aunt of Glenn and Ethel. Most of the time she was at the door to say hello. Lots of times she had me a piece of pie or apple stackcake.

One year I rode with Mr. Stamey. He let me out at the home of Kermit and Katherine Wells. They would walk to school

First row: Pauline Caldwell, Beatrice Kinsland, Mazie Kinsland, Louise Kinsland, Ruth Kinsland, Ruby Sanford, Charlie Massie, Bill Bishop. Second row: Avaline Gillett, Paul Sanford, Lucille Bishop, Ruby Massie, Lura Gillett, Mary Ruth Miller, Frances Bishop, Jody Massie. Third row: Ethel Caldwell, Effie Smith, Anna Bell Bishop, Eve Bishop, Alma Miller.

with me. Often Mr. Jerry Massie, grandfather of the Massie children, would be at the road with a horse for me to ride in the rain or mud.

The next year I bought a Model A Ford for $95.00. Roads were so bad I still had to walk part of the way or get Johnny Caldwell to bring my car to me. He would drive me back to the main road and walk back home. We had no driver's licenses back then so I drove even when I couldn't back a car.

One morning as I was coming across the narrow bridge across the Pigeon River, I met a man about half way. He really had the right of way. He was on the bridge first. I told him he would have to back his car, because I couldn't.

I had very few discipline problems. I don't mean to say we were perfect, neither teacher nor pupils. We made mistakes. We had conduct rules. Do right!

If anyone broke the rules there had to be punishment. This was done in various ways. The hill behind the school

27

was cleared and planted in roses and bushes by students working because of some misbehavior. Sometimes physical punishment seemed to be the only thing that helped. This was very few times.

What made the whole experience so gratifying was the cooperation of both parents and pupils.

I taught several pupils in my fourteen years of teaching, but I can truly say, I never had a more enjoyable time in my life.

As I think back, I am sure I made a lot of mistakes in my decisions about a lot of things. One thing that I am thankful for is that I had the privilege of teaching at Big Branch School. I think I made some lasting friends. I learned perhaps more than the pupils in a lot of things.

This is the story as told to me by Miss Bessie, our beloved teacher, with her permission for publication.

This school was in operation from 1927 through 1937. These were rewarding days in our lives.

Miss Bessie is a very special person and taught us also to let God have first place in our lives. By loving us and being our special friend, she taught us to love and respect each other.

The story as told by Mrs. Mildred Medford Wulff - 1985

In the fall of the year 1933, I set out walking one crisp morning from the home of Uncle Bill McCrary for the Big Branch School, perhaps one of the two remaining one-teacher schools.

There was a little girl at my side. My father had come with me to try and obtain the position and that was one of the *conditions*. "Your parents were both good teachers," stated Uncle Bill. "You can have the school position if my little granddaughter comes." (without Betty Jo Redmond, my load would have been less demanding for she was the only one in the first grade!)

What will it be like, I thought to myself? Well, before long we were in sight of the school, a typical frame building, set close to the road with a bank in the back. Not much place to play, I thought!

After meeting the scholars, I realized there'd probably not be too much time for playing. I had some students in each grade.

What I wouldn't give for that fifty-one-year-old grade and roll book! Then I could absolutely be sure as to the name of each ruddy-faced youngster. Poor! We were all poor, teachers and children together, but they were of a sweet disposition and eager to learn. That meant everything to an inexperienced nineteen year old girl with only one year of college!

Speaking of age, one of the pupils asked me my age, the first day of school. I was so naive I told him. That didn't help me any because the next day this student said right in the middle of geography, "My daddy said you're not old enough to teach anything!" This might have made discipline break down completely except for the fine way the boy's father stood behind me!

One incident I remember clearly. We were afraid of filling the stove with enough coal to get sufficient warmth because there was a generous crack which went almost all the way around the middle of the pot-bellied stove. I invited Mr. Jack Messer (Superintendent of Haywood County Schools) up. We made the circle bigger and handed him a book. Next, someone complained about having to sit too far back from the stove. As the iron became redder, Mr. Messer looked at me more apprehensively, and I believe suggested that it was unsafe for me to put future coal in. There was a new stove in the middle of the room come Monday morning.

I was having a time getting Paul Sanford ready for Junior High School and Betty Jo Redmond through the first grade.

However, those bright, rosy cheeked children all became fine citizens and good parents.

One time, one thing led to another, until a switching was needed, but if my memory serves me right, the young culprit broke the teacher's switch.

THE COUNTRY CHURCH

My memories of Crabtree Baptist Church

In the late 1920s and early 1930s my family lived in the Crabtree community. My parents, Flora and Garrett Kinsland, took us to the Crabtree Baptist Church.

After my father's death, we moved into the home of my grandparents, Dolly and Wiley Caldwell, at Big Branch.

My mother had small children at home so we walked with Grandpa. He walked slow and stopped to talk with neighbors. We nearly always arrived at church or back home before he did. We walked from Big Branch through the pastures and the edge of tobacco and corn fields. It was four miles.

We enjoyed our walks to church seeing all the flowers, birds, and trees and all the nature of God's beautiful world.

We girls became very close to each other because we were always together. Through hardships we learned to share and to cope with life.

We didn't go to church during the winter months. The snow was too deep and it was too cold. Sometimes in other seasons we got caught in rainstorms. Sometimes we would find a convenient shed or barn to stop off in. If not, we just got wet.

As I look back over the years, I realize the good teachers and pastors of the Crabtree Baptist Church had a big part in stabilizing our Christian lives. The teachers in the early years

The Country Church

influenced me in learning about God and how to become a Christian.

I gave my heart to God when I was twelve years old. I was baptized in the creek by the pastor, Doyle Miller.

Tommy Noland was the Sunday School Superintendent. His daughter, Ellen, became my friend. My sisters and I went home with them one Sunday for lunch. We went back to church for something special that night.

The card class at Crabtree Baptist stands out in my memory. The card class was located in a room on the right as we went into the church. The seats were made from blocks cut from trees. The blocks were worn slick from years of use. I don't remember what ages were in the card class.

The teacher gave us a card each Sunday. On the front of the card was a Bible verse and a picture relating to the story. On the back was the Bible story. We collected and saved our cards for several years. At home we played Sunday School by using the cards.

To go to the spring we walked down the hill through the woods. The men stood talking in groups at the spring. The

Crabtree Baptist Church

children just had fun going up and down the trail to the spring.

At one time we were given a New Testament for not missing a Sunday for a certain number of weeks. I was one of the lucky pupils who received one. That was my only Bible until I was married.

One of my early memories of the church came from the time I stood in the old cemetery and listened to the last rites at my father's funeral. After the service finished in the church, we had marched behind the casket to the graveyard. My mother was holding my sister Fannie. My grandma was leading my brother Garrett and my sister Beatrice. This left Mazie, Ruth, and me. We stood there, hand in hand, and listened to a group of people say, "She will have to put them in an orphanage home."

But my mother didn't put us in an orphanage. Fortunately for us, Grandma and Grandpa took us into their home.

A few years later, my Grandpa's funeral was the first one in the new Crabtree Baptist Church. Two years later, Grandma was buried beside him in the cemetery on the hill.

One of the highlights is going to Crabtree Baptist Church

on "decoration day" and being with the folks we grew up with. Crabtree Baptist is still one of our favorite churches.

We enjoy getting together with a group of people the evening before decoration at the cemetery. We reminisce about folks and families we know that are buried in the graveyard and we place flowers on our loved ones' graves.

I believe there is no sight more beautiful than seeing the sunset at the horizon of the cemetery on the hill at the Crabtree Baptist Church.

My mother, sisters, and I find ourselves at the beautiful setting so many times at sunset. It is so peaceful just standing there watching the sunset and listening to the sounds of the country. The beautiful mountains, the birds chirping, and the cattle grazing in the nearby pastures are sure signs of God's presence.

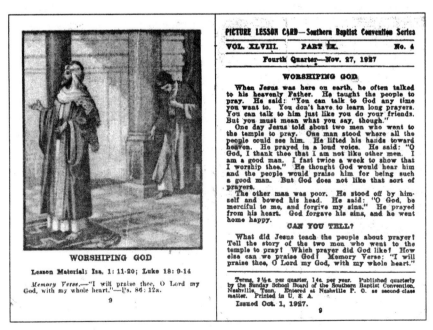

A Sunday School Card.

THE COMMUNITY COUNTRY DOCTOR

Our country doctor was Dr. Bob Walker. Dr. Walker lived in the Crabtree Community in Haywood County, NC. He served all the surrounding communities. He had a horse to travel on when I first remembered him. Later, he had a car.

His office was one room of his house. Sometimes when you went to see him you had to wait.

There was no telephone; so you rode a horse or walked to tell him of your family's illnesses.

I remember one time my brother, Gary, was very sick. My cousin, Glenn, took him to Dr. Walker on horseback.

One particular time that I remember visiting his office was when all us children had the itch. He had medicine on the shelves to give us, and we were told to go back to school.

Dr. Walker delivered all the babies in the surrounding communities. All my sisters, my brother, and I were delivered by Dr. Walker at home. He named my sister Mazie and her twin Daisy. I remember him coming to our home at Big Branch to deliver our younger sister. His fee was small and many times he was paid with vegetables, eggs, or country hams.

He registered all the babies he delivered in the Haywood County Courthouse. A short time later the parents would receive a birth certificate on a one cent postcard.

While he was in Waynesville one day, he had a heart attack and died in front of the Haywood County Courthouse. The community was sad because he was a well-loved doctor.

He is buried in the Crabtree Baptist Cemetery.

BIRTH OF MY YOUNGER SISTER

The year was 1936. It was during a bad time in our lives. My daddy was very sick. He had sold his car and his horse so we would have some extra money. During the summer he was a peddler. During the winter there was no extra money and the seventh baby was due. He had made arrangements with my uncle to get the community doctor when the time came.

The winter had been very cold. We got up very early one cold morning, and there was about five inches of snow on the ground. Every morning we went straight to the fireplace to get our shoes and socks. Daddy always put them by the fire to get warm.

Daddy told me and my sister that he didn't want us to be out in the cold, but we would need to get my uncle to go for the doctor. My sister was twelve years old and I was ten. While we were getting ready, he was getting the other children ready to take to the neighbor's home.

We knew we must hurry. So we ran as fast as we could. We didn't dare stop for we knew every minute counted.

During the two-mile walk through the woods and fields to my grandparents, my shoe sole came loose. It flopped up and down which delayed my running. When our shoe soles came loose, we wore a rubber can ring around it until Daddy or my uncle could get the last out and tack it back on.

When we arrived at my grandparents' house I was crying. Grandma realized that part of my crying was from being afraid because my parents were so anxious. I asked, "Will my mother be OK?" Also, I was crying because the sole off my shoe had come loose. She measured my foot with a stick and said she was going to get me some brogan shoes, shoes that would last. I begged her not to get those brogans because the children at school would laugh at me.

My uncle had to wait awhile on Dr. Walker. They barely got back on time. The neighbor had done a lot in preparation for the birth before they arrived.

Everything was fine with our new sister, and she was named after the neighbor because of her help with the delivery.

Before I left Grandma's, my uncle tacked my shoe sole back on and I told Grandma, "I don't need shoes. Daddy will let us go barefooted soon."

Grandma replied, "Your daddy won't let you go barefooted until May 1st." This was February 23rd.

Grandma went to town soon. She gave me the shoe box. I didn't want those old brogans, but I had to open them. To my surprise, they were slippers. I really gave Grandma a big hug for those beautiful slippers.

My sister's name was Fannie. She was a very special sister whom we all loved very much. My father passed away when Fannie was three months old. Fannie passed away in 1991 at age fifty-five.

WHAT IT WAS LIKE TO HAVE NO ELECTRICITY

In my early childhood there was no electricity. This meant no good lights. Our lights came from oil lamps with a wick. Each night the lamps were filled with oil, and wicks were trimmed. We carried lamps from room to room. To prepare our school work we used a lamp in the center of the kitchen table.

Since there were no outside lights, when you went outside you also carried a lantern that used oil and a wick.

Of course, with no electricity, heating the house had to be done by fireplace, wood stoves, and later, oil stoves.

We had no freezers, not even a refrigerator. So we stored our meats, milk, butter, and left over foods in covered pans in the springhouse. There was a trough where the water ran from the spring through the trough and out. If foods were used soon, they kept well enough that way.

We had no electric irons. We used the heavy black irons which were heated on top of the cook stove or in the coals in the fireplace. Most of the materials were cotton, so they had to be ironed. After a few rubbings over the clothes you replaced it with another hot iron.

We had a battery operated radio with an outside aerial. We were far from the radio stations, so there was a lot of static. No television!

No electric stoves. We used wood stoves. This created a job keeping wood just for cooking.

No appliances, mixers, toasters, popcorn poppers, microwaves, blenders, curling irons, razors, hair dryers, etc.

No hot water heaters. We heated water on top of the stove in tubs for washing clothes in the winter time. We heated water in a black iron pot outside in the summer for washing clothes (more wood needed).

Also there was no clothes dryer. We hung the clothes outside to dry.

What, no baths! Yes, we had baths by heating water in a tub on top of the kitchen stove. When we got baths we closed off the kitchen door and took our baths in the kitchen in the wash tub. Why not take a bath in the bathroom? Because we had no bathroom, we used outside toilets.

Right: a trough in a springhouse used for cooling stored food. Bottom left: a woodstove for cooking and bottom right: an outside toilet.

SIGNS, BELIEFS, AND HOME REMEDIES OF THE OLDER FOLKS

My grandparents could neither read nor write, so they went by signs and beliefs.

During my early childhood in the 1930s until my grandparents passed away, we heard all the ways that they thought would help them in life.

My grandmother and mother would not make kraut, pickled beans, and pickled corn unless the signs were from the head to the heart. With my mother's supervision, that is the way we make kraut now.

My grandfather was a firm believer in weather signs. These are some of the signs that I have heard him talk about.

Bad Weather

> Wooly worms with a heavy coat
> When the moon was lying on its point
> When hickory nuts had a thick shell
> For every fog in August there would be snow
> If the snow was cross-legged it would be deep
> Tramping fire sounds, there would be snow
> If it's cloudy and the smoke rises, it will snow
> During a wind storm, if leaves turn over it will rain

The weather was told by sunsets
If the sun was shining while it was raining, it would rain again the next day.

Planting was done by signs

Plant beans on Good Friday
Plant potatoes when the moon was dark in March
Plant corn when the dogwoods were in bloom
If you cut weeds in the right sign, you could get rid of them, otherwise you couldn't.

The time of day was told exactly by the position of the sun.

Home Remedies For Pain and Sickness

Use chimneysoot in the wound for bleeding
Use a small amount of kersone oil for bleeding
To help measles, use sassafras or spice tree tea
For a burn, put cold water on it to draw out the steam
Raw potatoes to draw out burning steam
For a cold in the chest, use a poultice of camphor and turpentine
Boneset tea for colds
Eat honey and vinegar for colds
Tea from wintergreen for colds
For colic, put an asafetida bag around the baby's neck
For indigestion, use soda and water
For croup, groundhog oil
For croup, make a poultice out of onions and turpentine
For ear aches, blow smoke from a cigarette in the ear
Use catnip tea to calm baby to make it sleep
For bee stings, cover with wet snuff
For poison ivy use buttermilk, vinegar, and salt
For itch, use mixture of sulphur and lard
Hold your head back to stop a bleeding nose
Epson salt and very hot water for swelling
For sore throat, gargle with salt and vinegar water
For toothache use drops of vanilla
To get rid of warts, steal a dishcloth and bury it
Make a candy from Jerusalem Oak to get rid of worms

Then along came Rose Bud, Cloverine, and Vick's salves.
These are some of the home remedies that I can remember. I'm sure there are many more. Most of the salves, tea mixes, etc. were stored on the mantle (fireboard).

THE COUNTRY STORES

We saved our eggs to sell at the country store. The needed items purchased with the egg or chicken money were items such as sugar, black pepper, salt, baking powder, soda, and others plus Garrett's or Burton snuff for Mama and Grandma. Occasionally, there would be extra pennies or sometimes we had to pay the extra money on the charge account. Sometimes there wouldn't hardly be enough money from the eggs, but John Haney would charge the balance.

When we had extra pennies, we would purchase one-cent BB Bat suckers or get five silver bells or five pieces of candy for a penny. John Haney never let us leave the store unless he gave us a few pieces of candy. This made the trip more enjoyable.

The eggs had to be carried carefully. We would pack straw in the basket around the eggs. If we had to carry an old hen, their legs were tied together, and sometimes they squawked all the way to the store. We were embarrassed to carry them, so we couldn't wait until they were taken from us and put on the scales to be weighed.

Around the store you would see men buying pieces of a big slab of tobacco. They would say they wanted ten or fifteen cents worth. There was always someone hanging around drinking the drinks like Orange Crush, strawberry and grape Nehi or Cokes (all called dopes).

We took our time in returning home. There was this special place where we sat on the rocks by the branch and just enjoyed eating our candy. Sometimes the BB Bat sucker would last all the way home.

It didn't take much to make us happy (just a little candy).

THE JOHN HANEY STORE

The John Haney store was located on a bank right off the Hyder Mountain Road. The store was in a curve and almost in the middle of Hyder Mountain in Haywood County, North Carolina.

The store was owned and operated by John Haney and his wife Cynthia Clark Haney. The store's opening date was in the early 1920s and closed in the early 1940s.

These are some of the memories of John Haney's granddaughter, Ruby Price Best, and his grandsons, Ray Haney and Ed Smith.

Grandpa was crippled, something called "white swelling." This didn't stop him from performing his many duties. He was not only the store keeper, he was a farmer, blacksmith, miller, and he traded cows and western horses.

He bought the horses untrained and someone broke them in for him. He had sheds and stalls to keep the cows and horses in.

In the corn mill, he would take part of the turning of corn from grinding the corn into meal. He used the corn to feed the livestock and he ground some into meal to sell.

He could not read nor write. When a customer needed something charged, he would ask them to put their name and the amount on the book. He trusted everyone, but there were lots of accounts that didn't get paid. He had no trouble

Cynthia and John Haney, owners of the Hyder Mountain Country Store.

counting his money and making change. He had his own ways of figuring out how to manage the store.

There was a long porch across the front of the store. The porch was a gathering place where everyone got all the news and where they chewed their tobacco. If they didn't have a homemade twist of tobacco in the overall pocket, Grandpa sold them a piece of the large plug of tobacco. If they wanted ten, fifteen, or twenty-five cents worth, he would judge how big a piece to cut off.

There was nearly always time to have a big dope. The dopes were grape, orange Nehi, and colas. Drinks were a nickel each.

In the winter months the crowd gathered around the pot-bellied stove in the store to hear the latest news.

Grandpa was called "Uncle John." His favorite name for the children and women was "Honney." If someone would ask him for credit he would say, "Doggone, I growneys, Honney, I have so much on my book now." After being persuaded that they needed credit, he would say, "Honney, what do you need?" He never turned anyone down.

He bought eggs and chickens to resell. The chickens were carried to the store with a string tied around their legs. He hung the chickens on the scales by the string to weigh them. He would know where the scales registered and he would determine if he owed a quarter, fifty cents or seventy-five cents. A guy with a truck by the name of McDowell picked up the chickens. He had chicken crates to put them in.

The store supplied every thing you could think of—things like overalls, shirts, cloth, buttons, thread, needles, snuff, tobacco, coffee, sugar, salt, candles, pencils, tablets, nails, and lots of things the farmers needed and many more items.

One thing that stands out in mind was the candy counter. There were lots of kinds of the BB Bat suckers for one cent. Five silver bells cost one cent.

There was a hand-cranked gas tank and an oil barrel for kerosene oil.

People traveling through from Fines Creek to Clyde or Canton would travel the Hyder Mountain Road. They would be on horse back or have horses and wagons. Grandma and Grandpa's was a convenient place to stop and spend the night. The horses would need to stop and rest by then and sometimes needed shoeing. Grandpa would feed them and shoe them if needed. Grandma saw that they got fed supper and breakfast. Then they would buy loads of staple goods for the home.

We remember Grandpa getting his first car. No one knew how to drive. No one needed licenses either. Grandpa got in the car and very soon lost control. He didn't know what else to do except holler, "Whoa!"

It was a pleasure for them to be with and serve the people. The country store was their life.

THE TAFT FERGUSON STORE

Mary and Taft Ferguson owned the Ferguson Store at Crabtree, close to the entrance of Big Branch in Haywood County. The store operated from the early 1920s to the year 1943, and the store closed due to the ill health of Taft.

Talking to Kate Clark, their daughter, this was part of the past that she could remember.

Flour was sold in twenty-four pound cloth bags for seventy-five cents a bag. The bags were used later for making curtains and clothing.

Mary and Taft Ferguson

Kate said they bought eggs from the customers for one cent each (twelve cents a dozen) and chickens for five cents a pound. The chickens were placed in chicken crates and a guy picked them up every week. The guy was a Mr. McDowell.

Cigarettes were fifteen cents a package. They sold Winston, Camel and several other brands. Smoking tobacco came in cans by Prince Albert and Bull Durham. Licenses were necessary to sell tobacco.

Sugar was bought in bulk (100 pound sacks). Coffee was sold for about fifteen cents a pound. It was weighed and

45

ground one pound at a time. Then we put it in bags (pokes) and tied twine around the top.

Soft drinks were sold for five cents. They were called dopes or big RC's. We had an ice box to keep them cold, and we got ice several times a week in the hot summer months. No ice was required in the winter months.

Gasoline was hand pumped for twelve cents a gallon. The kerosene oil (lamp oil) was also sold by the gallon. You know we didn't have electricity.

The first chocolate candy that I remember selling in the store was the chocolate drop with the white center. We also sold horehound and peppermint stick candy.

Some of the other things she remembered them selling were buttons, needles, thread, cloth, overalls, oil cloth for table covers, lamps, lamp wicks, lanterns, horse shoes, and bags of cattle feed.

There was also canvas cloth for tobacco beds, nails, staples, seeds, chewing tobacco, snuff, teaberry chewing gum, castor oil, and Vick's salves, etc.

We asked if she bought country hams from the customers. She didn't remember, but she said they did sell them. They sold about everything that anyone needed.

A lot of people bought on credit. Some accounts went until tobacco was sold and then paid. Lots of accounts never got paid.

My daddy farmed and worked in the store. Mama helped him run the store and the children helped, too. We all helped with the farming and the garden. We had cows to milk.

Someone told me recently that Peggy Medford had our old weight scales. I wish we had kept the scales, the scoops, the gas tank, coffee grinder, and lots of other items. We didn't know they would be of interest to our families later, nor how valuable they would become.

Times have really changed. Sometimes I think times were better back then. People had time to visit, go to church, and help with the sick. We were all very poor, everyone. We didn't know the difference. We never went hungry and we had enough clothes to wear.

FOOD PREPARATIONS OF THE EARLY DAYS

When we were growing up in the late 1920s and the early 1930s, Grandma, Grandpa, and Mama grew, preserved, buried, or canned everything they could so the family would have plenty of food.

Cabbage, potatoes, turnips, and apples were gathered and buried in the ground for winter months. After digging the hole, straw was packed in the bottom and on the sides. The vegetables and apples were put in the hole with more straw on top. Dirt and rocks were placed over all that. Then there was tin or some other item to cover the hole to prevent rain from going in.

Apples were dried, canned, or smoked. Some apples were sliced and dried in the sun, then packed in flour sacks for storage. The smoked apples were smoked over coals with sulphur burning. The apples were placed in a basket for smoking and placed in crock jars and kept cool.

Canning was still a new thing in those days. Corn was still hard to keep in canning. There had to be a lot of experiments in canning corn. Corn was made into hominy, ground into meal for cornbread and mush, or ground coarse for grits.

Hogs were raised and killed for meat, like streaked meat for frying, country hams, fatback, canned, cracklings for shortening bread, backbones and ribs. Sausage was canned. Lard was rendered and put into lard buckets.

The large pots and pans used in putting-up food. The strainers were used constanly in the blanching and scalding of vegetables.

When hog killing time came, several days were set aside to render the lard, make sausage, souse meat, livermush, cure hams, and can the shoulders.

The chickens provided meat for frying, making stew, dumplings, and for eggs in cooking and to use in baking cakes and puddings.

Chickens helped meet another need. The chickens were sold and money was used to buy sugar, salt, coffee, and the extras that were needed.

Cows provided milk, buttermilk, cream, butter, and meat.

Churning was a chore. The cream was placed in jars to thicken, then put in the churn. The dash was pushed up and down until the butter was formed. The butter was removed from the buttermilk, salted, and pressed into the buttermold. Then both butter and buttermilk were put in the cold water in the springhouse. This kept them very cold and prevented souring. The extra milk was fed to the hogs.

The beans were canned. Beans were also strung on a thread and dried. These were called "leather britches" or "shucky beans." After they dried they were placed in flour sacks for winter use. There were also shelled beans and shelled blackeyed peas, saved for winter.

All berries such as strawberries, blackberries, cherries, dewberries, and huckleberries were canned. Bushels of peaches were bought and canned. Apples were made into applesauce. Jelly and jams were made from berries, apples, and peaches.

After the frost, fox grapes that grew wild were gathered to make jelly. Persimmons were not good until after the frost came on them.

We also gathered nuts from the wild including black walnuts, white walnuts, hickory nuts, hazelnuts, chestnuts, and chinquapins. All except chestnuts and chinquapins would keep all winter.

All these berries and nuts are not as plentiful now as then. It seems God provided all our needs. All the families took all the plentiful foods provided by God and used them.

We canned mustard and turnip greens. In the spring months we ate poke salad, cressy greens, and branch lettuce.

Vegetables were pickled as well as canned. They were placed in crock jars for the pickling process and storage. There were always pickled beans and kraut and pickles made from cucumbers. Beets were pickled and canned.

A mixture of vegetables was used to make soup, which was also canned.

We grew cane to make into molasses. We cut the cane just before frost, then boiled it at different stages until the juice became thick. The foam was skimmed off, and the molasses was put into buckets for storage.

We also ate wild meat such as rabbit and squirrel cooked with gravy. Occasionally we had mutton.

The men were always fishing, and we had plenty of fish. Their special fish was mountain trout.

In the fall pumpkins and candyroasters were gathered and stored in a cool place. These were made into pies.

We rolled sweet potatoes and green tomatoes in newspaper to be stored. Onions were hung in the shed to dry out.

Jars of fruits and vegetable, canned for winter use.

Honey was always on the table. Not only did the men-folk use the honey from their bee hives, they scouted the woods in search of bee swarms.

When they found a bee swarm, they marked the tree and went back later for the honey. The honey was kept in quart jars for storage.

The men, women, and children all worked to save and preserve the food. Not many people went hungry. Some of the people that were less fortunate were widows with small children. The neighbors shared eggs, milk, butter, and food with each other.

The women delighted in showing off all the cans in the cellar and all the crock jars with smoked fruit, kraut, pickled beans, and pickles. They exchanged recipes for canning and preserving.

Left, leather britches, right, dried red peppers and handmade corn grater.

They all delighted in using the foods to make delicious meals. The house was always filled with an aroma of the good foods cooking. These memories linger on.

METHODS OF PRESERVING LEATHER BRITCHES OR SHUCKY BEANS

The beans were strung on a twine or heavy thread by using a needle. The thread was run through the middle of the bean. Then they were hung up in the kitchen to dry. After they dried they were placed in a flour sack to keep the dust off.

To cook leather britches, they were thoroughly washed, placed in boiling water with a hunk of fat meat and salt, and cooked just like dried beans.

DRIED RED PEPPER

To prepare for making the sausage when the hogs were killed, the farmer's wives dried red pepper. The red pepper was dried by running a thread with a needle through the long, thin pods of pepper and hung up to dry.

51

SAGE

Sage was a must in making the sausage. The sage was grown and dried.

ONIONS

The farmer's wife had to be prepared to cook. Since they didn't have stores to run out to, they saved and preserved everything they would need in cooking.

After onions were dug they were hung up to dry. Then they were placed in a dry place and every time they needed the onions for cooking or to have with a pot of dried beans, they had it.

SWEET POTATOES

To grow sweet potatoes, there had to be a special type of ground. On the farm where we lived, there was a hilly spot of land which nearly always became the spot to grow sweet potatoes.

My grandfather bought sweet potato slips from a Bradshaw guy who live in Ironduff. They bought both red and white slips.

To save the sweet potatoes for winter use, they rolled each sweet potato in a separate piece of newspaper and kept them in a dry place. In our home, they were placed in an upstairs bedroom.

Many a time we came home from school and found left over from lunch, baked sweet potatoes in the warmer on the old wood cook stove.

My mother and grandmother fried sweet potatoes and made sweet potato pies.

HOMINY

To make hominy, the drippings of lye made from ashes, water, and the hard dry kernels of shelled corn was used.

The big grains of corn were placed in the iron wash pot with the lye and water. The corn was boiled until it began to crack and the husk started coming off. The corn was rinsed several times in cold spring water to get rid of the husk and the lye. The hominy was boiled again for several hours in the

Kitchen things

wash pot until it became tender. Then it was stored in crock jars in the cellar with all the other jars of vegetables.

The neighbors always shared in the hominy because it didn't last long without spoiling.

SMOKED FRUIT

Smoked fruit, as our family called it, was made in a very special way.

Just the right kind of apples were used. They were peeled, cored, and quartered, then placed in a basket. There was a makeshift way to secure the basket for smoking the apples. The basket handle was secured by running a pole through it. Then the pole was placed across the backs of two straight chairs. Underneath the basket was a pan with burning sulphur and across the top of the basket was a heavy cloth. The cloth was not allowed to touch the apples. The apples needed all the benefit of the smoke from the burning sulphur. This technique would bleach the apples.

The smoking was done on the porch because of the bad smell. Sulphur was added to the pan often. It took about six to eight hours to complete this job.

The apples were stored in a crock jar which was covered tightly. The jar was placed in the cellar with the other jars of vegetables. The smoked fruit was either stewed or baked and the family enjoyed it.

SHOE REPAIRING AND SHOE BUYING

Shoes (slippers) were bought in the spring for Sunday shoes and sometimes in the fall for school and at Christmas time. With Mama and Daddy and six children to buy shoes for, it took a lot of money to purchase eight pairs of shoes.

My daddy was a peddler and managed his money well, but $5.00 to $8.00 for shoes for the whole family was a lot of money.

Sometimes just wearing shoes on Sunday we made out well during the summer months. We started going barefooted the first day of May and except for Sunday, we didn't want shoes on our feet.

To buy shoes, Daddy cut sticks and measured our feet with the sticks. He carried these to the shoe store and bought the shoes just a little longer.

We were thrilled to receive the new slippers and to wear them the first few times. Even though we were excited over wearing the slippers the first time, we dreaded it because I don't think we ever had a pair of shoes that didn't blister our feet. In fact, by the time we arrived at church our feet were already blistered. As soon as we got away from church we carried our slippers back home. By the next Sunday, our feet would be blistered all over again and we went through the same process for several Sundays.

Shoes weren't made as good as they are now. Soon the threads wore out in the soles and until my Uncle Johnny and

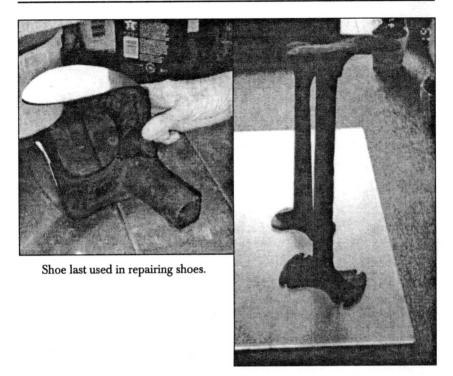

Shoe last used in repairing shoes.

Daddy could mend the shoes, we wore a rubber can ring around them to keep them from flopping up and down. I must admit it was very embarrassing to wear the can rings to school like that. But in our one-room school several of the other children also occasionally needed to wear them that way.

Every family was prepared to mend shoes. Each family had a shoe last and shoe tacks. The shoe last had two parts—the stand and the part that went in the shoe. Daddy had a smaller one that fit on the stand to repair the children's shoes. The last was made of very heavy iron and always sat in the corner until it was needed. They couldn't put the thread back in, so they nailed shoe tacks around the soles and many a time the tacks would hurt our feet. It kept Daddy busy pulling the tacks out that would hurt our feet.

After my Daddy's death, Uncle Johnny was continually repairing our slippers. This was just one way to survive in the days of the past.

FIREPLACE CRUCIAL ROLE IN CHILDHOOD

What an important thing the fireplace was during my childhood.

The fireplace provided the heat for the house. Grandpa and his sons cut big logs of wood. Some were cut in pieces and some were large for the back log. Then there was the dry wood to keep it kindled.

The fire did not go out in the winter months. Grandpa saw to that. He got up during the night and put more logs on the fire.

Inside the fireplace were iron poles with a hook on them. The purpose of these poles was to but black kettles loaded with soup beans, roasts, back bones, and ribs and many other foods for good cooking.

Eggs were rolled in wet papers or wet corn shucks and put in the coals to bake. There were the ears of corn rolled in wet papers or wet corn shucks, also for baking. Potatoes baked in the coals were very good. We raked them out with the fireplace poker.

In the oven pan we made huge cakes of corn pone. The cakes of bread were about four or five inches thick. Coals were placed around and on top of the lid. What delicious corn pone it was. Sometimes we made shortening bread in the same fashion.

The popcorn we grew was our favorite. Before we got a

This was the way my grandfather's mother prepared their meals.

cornpopper with a long handle, Uncle Johnny made the popper by punching holes in the bottom, sides, and lid of a lard bucket. He held the bucket over the fire by the rod he had made. He cut holes opposite each other near the top of the bucket and ran the rod through the bucket popper.

We also used the fireplace for ironing. We set irons in the coals to heat. We had to hold the irons with thick cloths. In a few minutes the irons were cold and the process started all over again.

To stay warm on cold days we took turns standing near the fire. We stood so close the fire nearly scorched our legs.

We cleaned the fireplace every other day. There were ashes galore, but even they were useful. The ashes were used in making hominy and soap and were also placed around the bean and potato plants to kill bugs.

The chimneys were made of rocks and mud. The upstairs of the old log house was warm because a lot of heat rose up the chimney. It was not the best heat in the world, but we survived.

I can almost see the straight chairs sitting by the fireplace, and the shovel and the poker sitting against the rock chimney. There was also a handmade broom sitting nearby to keep the ashes swept up.

The mantle, or fireboard, was a safe place for many medicines including Epsom salts, castor oil, Rose Bud salve, bonset tea mix, groundhog oil, sulphur, dry mustard, dried catnip, Vick's pneumonia salves, asafetida, Watkins Linament, and Vaseline, also many other items like razor blades or a box of buttons.

We sat by the fire at night telling ghost stories and just relaxing with the family. We also played checkers and shelled the corn for the meal by the fire. This corn shelling took place every Friday night.

The crackling sounds and the popping sounds that came from the fire were all different depending upon the type of wood we were burning. There was this particular sound that the fire made. Grandpa would say, "The fire is tramping snow."

GRANDMA'S DUCKS (THE QUACKERS)

What a beautiful sight it was as you approached the duck pond with all the ducks swimming and, it seems like, all quacking at the same time.

The water for the duck pond came from the mountain spring, through a heavy stream to fill the duck pond with the clear sparkling water.

There were just enough bushes and large rocks to make a beautiful setting for the stream and the pond.

Up and down the stream banks at our country home in the cove at Big Branch were all the ducks and drakes.

Grandpa had made duck coops for them to sleep in, but they chose to sleep on the stream banks and around the pond.

They also had their nests on the banks of the stream. We would go out early every morning to gather the big eggs. They always laid their eggs at dawn. If they laid eggs in the nest we would leave them. Soon they would be setting on the eggs and before long we would have lots of baby ducks. A lot of the mother ducks were white. The baby ducks were yellow.

It was fun to watch the mother ducks teaching the ducklings to swim in their nice big pond.

We would try catching the baby ducks to play with, but the mother duck always came after us. Occasionally, we were able to catch one. Oh, how we loved to hold them.

This is the rock where Grandma sat to pluck the feathers from her ducks. The pond was close by.

We enjoyed feeding the ducks. They came out of the pond flapping their wings and hurrying to us for food. With their quacking, they seemed to be telling all the ducks that it was feeding time.

I can almost see grandma in her long dress and long apron gathered at the waist, her hair in a bun, pulling on her bonnet to go outside.

She would gather up feed sacks and a bucket of shelled corn. Then she would hunt for a clean spot with a convenient rock for sitting on, and we would be ready to catch the ducks for her.

She would tell us to put down just a few grains of corn to catch a duck. After running and grabbing, we would manage to catch one. Grandma would sit on the rock. She took the duck, turned its head under her arm, and plucked off the feathers. We stood holding the feed sacks for her to put feathers in. The ducks were quacking all the time.

Then we would try again and again until we would catch another duck. We proceeded to finish catching and plucking the feathers until every one had been "picked" as grandma would say.

The little fine feathers next to the skin were called "down." These were the best for making pillows.

Grandma made the pillow covers and feather ticks out of ticking. This cloth was white with a blue stripe and very sturdy. She sewed all her seams several times, so the sewing would be secured.

Many times during the summer and fall the pillows and feather beds would be aired and sunned.

Sometimes the duck provided us with more than pillows. Many times we had roasted duck for a Sunday dinner or a very special meal.

The ducks were a part of our everyday life. They were just a small part of life that went on when living on the farm. We really enjoyed the ducks.

Grandma Caldwell and chickens

CHILDREN'S CHORES

Everyone helped on the farm. Mama had told us when we went to live with Grandma and Grandpa that we would help out with the chores.

In the spring when the garden was planted, our job would be to keep the hens and her baby chicks (dibbies) from scratching up the seeds. The mama hen would scratch and then cluck to the chicks, and they would cheep and soon the seeds were all eaten up.

Then a sudden heavy rain would come up, and Grandma would tell us to go in the fields, hunt the hens and chicks and get them home because the tall, wet weeds would drown them.

Churning was a children's job. The milk had set by the kitchen stove in a crock jar, getting clabbered and ready to churn. Mama or Grandma placed it in the churn, and we pushed the dash up and down until we had butter and buttermilk. They removed the butter, salted it, pressed it in the butter molds, and placed it in covered pans. Then the buttermilk was poured in buckets and carried to the spring house to keep fresh.

We hoed in the corn and tobacco fields. We picked berries. Our hands were just right to fit in the jars to wash. The wash tub was full of warm, soapy water for washing and a tub of clear water for rinsing the cans to be filled with fruits and vegetables.

Every Monday morning was wash day. In the summer and before we went to school, we carried water to fill the reservoir on the stove and two tubs of water on the stove to heat for washing. If the washing was to be done outside, we filled iron wash pots with water for boiling clothes. We helped rub them on the wash board and we helped iron with the black irons heated on top of the stove or inside the fireplace.

Every Friday night we all gathered around the fireplace to shell corn. Saturday mornings, Grandpa either took the horse and wagon filled with bags of shelled corn to the mill for making meal, or he carried one sack if that was all that was needed.

Carrying in wood seemed to be a children's job, also. We kept wood in the stove box in the kitchen and piled up by the fireplace in the main part of the house. We also put stacks of wood on the porch.

Our job was to bring the cows home to be milked. We played along as we went and enjoyed the beautiful things of nature.

We were just the right size to stoop over and help pick beans and tomatoes. In the fall we picked blackeyed peas. We carried those in the feed sacks and we all sat by the fire shelling them. There would be several bags of shelled peas for winter use. We helped shuck corn if the corn shucker missed the shucks. We helped pick up potatoes after they were dug.

These were just a few chores that we helped with. It would seem that this was a miserable job. Actually, we were used to it and it was what was necessary for living. I can't say we hated the job because I don't think we did. We went on with our life without grumbling. We learned how to cope, how to save, and to do jobs as they should be done.

BOTTOMING CHAIRS

Before my cousin Sherman Justice passed away, we had a conversation on bottoming chairs. Sherman was in his late eighties, but his mind was very bright on this subject.

Sherman learned the craft from his father, Tommy Justice, at a very early age. He went with his father to gather the splits and to learn how when he was just old enough to follow him.

Sherman and Tommy bottomed chairs all over Crabtree and Fines Creek. They were paid a very small fee for their work, or sometimes they were paid with items such as honey, molasses, etc.

A sixty-year-old cane bottom chair.

Sherman said he went scouting in the woods early in the spring to find straight saplings from hickory or white oak. He preferred white oak. Then when the sap was just right he went back to get the bark for making splits.

Sherman Justice stands behind his father, Tommy Justice. This photo was taken about the time Sherman started following his daddy to the woods, learning the trade of bottoming chairs. Sherman crafted the bottom of the chair on the adjacent page.

He would skin and husk the outside and make the splits with a special, very sharp knife. He said he must be very careful to make the splits straight.

Sometimes he would have to soak the bark because it dried out so fast. Soaking made it easy to work with. He tried to work the splits up the same day he gathered them.

He would weave the splits very close and tight together. On the front of the chair he would put one split under the straight across split. The next one would be woven in two times under the next two splits. Then he would go over instead of under, making a sturdy, neat bottom. He always used a tack to secure the first and last split.

He said many of the chairs would be homemade. Most of them were just straight chairs bought from stores. My mother and I still have some of these chairs. These chairs were bottomed by Sherman sixty years ago. If chairs were taken care of they lasted many years.

Bottoming chairs had a special knack. Not many people learned this knack. Sherman and his father were considered the best. It was a delight to watch them work with the chairs.

Sherman was always trading knives. He always had some of the best knives. What time he was sitting around, he was sharpening knives for everyone.

Bottoming chairs is one of the specialties of days gone by.

THEIR FIRST CAR

What was it like to own your first car?

My Uncle Johnny told me this story about wanting a car so badly and how he worked out the money for the car.

Johnny's friend, Goble McCrary, owned a T Model Ford. So did his father, Bill McCrary. He had ridden with Goble and would have given anything to be in the driver's seat.

Jerry Massie asked Johnny if he could drive. Johnny told him he was sure he could. However, he hadn't driven before. Jerry said, "If I can get Bill to loan his car to me, would you take me to Canton?" He said he sure would. Jerry approached Bill about loaning him his car. Bill was hesitant, but he told Johnny if he was sure he could drive, then Jerry could borrow the car.

Finally Johnny was in the driver's seat. What a great feeling. He had watched other drivers and he had no trouble. By now, he had the fever so bad he must get himself a car.

At this time no driver's license was required.

Goble told Johnny he would like to have a newer car and if he would give him $140 he would sell him the car.

Johnny started planning to own the car. He had a tobacco crop which was ready to cut and cure. He could hardly wait until it was cured to class it out and tie into hands for the market.

The Massie boys, Hubert Wells, my father Garrett Kinsland, and others had cars by now. Garrett and Goble had been

A car from the days when the car salesman came to you.

letting Johnny drive. He had learned the parts of the car and how to repair it. It was very exciting.

When a car salesman found someone interested in buying a car, he came into the rural areas and demonstrated the car. A car salesman knew Miss Bessie McClure was in desperate need of a car. She had walked through the snow and ice to get to her job of teaching at the one-room school at Big Branch. So, he came to the school and demonstrated the car to her. This convinced her that she needed the car.

While she was learning to drive, she asked Johnny to meet her at the entrance of Big Branch Road and drive her to the school. When the bell rang for school to be out, Johnny was waiting to take her back to the main road.

The Big Branch Road was in bad condition. The road was routed out. When it snowed or rained the road was very slick. Johnny said he put heavy chains on the car to pull out of the mud.

Miss Bessie welcomed the chance for Johnny to help her with the car because she could not back up yet. One day she met a car on the narrow bridge at the Taft Ferguson store. She

T. J. Mason's car.

just stopped and told the driver that he would have to back up because she couldn't.

The tobacco market in Clyde finally opened and Johnny took his tobacco as soon as possible. After the tobacco sold, Johnny arrived home too late to make the deal with Goble.

He was lying in bed, thinking tomorrow he would be the owner of the car. He heard and saw someone raising the window and the guy was half way in when Johnny scared him off. Johnny was making so much noise getting his gun that the burglar fled. Johnny was sure the burglar was after his money.

As soon as he could the next morning, he made the trade for the car. He was now the happy owner of the T Model car.

He had to use more of his tobacco money to buy tires for the car.

He and Marshall Sanford had a job getting out "acid wood." They didn't make much money but this enabled them to buy gas for the car.

Saturday afternoons and Sundays they drove to Waynesville, mostly to show off the car. In Waynesville they would see different cars and they loved talking to owners of other cars.

RIDING IN A RUMBLE SEAT

On Saturday and Sunday afternoons Daddy took us for rides in the T Model car with the rumble seat.

We lived at Lake Junaluska, and our grandparents lived in the Crabtree section of Haywood County.

This one particular time was on a Sunday afternoon. First we rode to the Balsam Fish Hatchery. We enjoyed the fish and trying to catch the little prairie dogs. These were beautiful little animals. I guess they weighed one half to two pounds, and they were about ten inches long. These were in the park at the fish hatchery. When we chased them they went into holes in the ground. This was our favorite place to go.

Daddy put my sister Ruth and me in the rumble seat. Mama, two small children, and Daddy were in the front seat. We were told not to stand up in the rumble seat, just sit still.

We arrived at the fish hatchery and played a good long while with the dogs.

Daddy announced, "It's time to go to Grandma and Grandpa's." He put Ruth and me in the rumble seat. As we went down the road, the rumble seat closed up on us. Fortunately, we had arms and hands inside. We were very frightened. It was dark in there. We cried and beat on the car, but for a while we were unnoticed.

Daddy looked in the mirror to check on us and saw that the seat was closed up. He got us out, and we begged him not to put us back in the rumble seat. He assured us everything would be OK. Again he said, "Sit still." Our heads were hardly to the top of the opening. We kept trying to decide if we were nearly to grandma and grandpa's house. Nothing looked familiar and we were worried about the door closing on us again. Suddenly, we made a turn and we figured we were there. We looked up and we were under the big Bellflower and Buff apple trees. Those belonged to grandma and grandpa. We were safe at last.

THE BIG SNOW
March 17, 1936

The wind was blowing. The snow was falling heavy and fast. No one expected the snow to amount to anything, due to the time of the year. However, it was accumulating fast.

Johnny and Daddy each had a battery radio. They were both listening to the weather warnings. Johnny and Glenn (our relatives) decided they had better come to saw and chop wood for our family because Daddy was sick. They cut until all the logs and limbs were ready. We children helped to carry it and stack it on the porch. Johnny and Glenn headed home in a blizzard. The snow was already deep. Since there was no way to know if they got there safely, we wondered and worried. The weather reports kept saying, "Heavy, heavy snows with drifts were on the way."

Bob Bishop (our neighbor) kept coming to our house to hear the weather report since the battery was dead for his radio.

I was only ten years old, but I could tell by their anxiety that a big snow storm was coming.

Our teacher, Mrs. Bessie McClure Evans, closed school at 10 a.m. She walked through the snow storm to the main highway to meet her ride. Carroll Morrow had borrowed her car and drove to the Crabtree school approximately four miles away where he taught. Mr. Morrow's school also let out early. He had trouble with the chains and he picked Miss Bessie up later. Her coat was covered completely and frozen

71

stiff. She lived at Clyde so to avoid too many miles in traveling, she took a short cut and let Mr. Morrow walk part of the way home. Her windshield wipers wouldn't work, so she had to ride with her head out the window to see how to drive.

The road was being scraped and several cars were stalled. She traveled on, getting home by 5 p.m.

After Daddy finished feeding the hogs and the milking was done, we all settled in waiting on the blizzard to continue.

Soon the dog was barking because the snow was covering the door of his house. Daddy moved the dog and his house to the porch. All night we could hear the wind and wondered how deep the snow was.

Before dawn Daddy was up, and at daybreak he got the shock of his life. There was not a bush in sight nor a fence post and no way to get to the spring. Fence posts were three feet tall and the snow was deeper than that.

Daddy started melting snow for water use. Soon he started digging his way to the barn to milk the cow. At 4 p.m he got to the barn. Daddy was six feet tall and we could barely see the top of this head. With all the shoveling, the snow was still waist deep in his trail. The snow had to be melted and carried for the livestock to drink.

It was very exciting and also very scary, knowing that we were completely closed in. We were afraid to make a few steps from the house. We were certain we would get lost in the snow. We couldn't see the neighbors.

A neighbor's flock of sheep was caught in the snow in the hills of the pasture. After a hard struggle they made their way to the sheep and rolled a snow ball from the top of the pasture. This snowball made a trail to the barn for the sheep. What a huge snowball is was! It was several weeks before the snowball melted.

Daddy kept listening to the weather news. The snowdrifts were ten to fifteen feet deep elsewhere. Before the snow melted, Daddy had to use planks off of the barn for wood.

School was out for a week, and it was a week before we saw Johnny and Glenn again.

Since this was the year of 1936 we were ready for winter

weather. We didn't have to depend on oil or electricity for heating. There was no electricity yet. We depended on fireplaces and wood stoves for heat.

There were very few cars, so we didn't worry about traveling. We also didn't worry about getting eggs, milk and bread from the grocery store. We had our own. Biscuits and corn bread were the bread, not a loaf of bread. We used our canned goods and meat from the smoke house. We had plenty of potatoes, pumpkins, and dried apples to get us through the storm.

We didn't see the mail man for a week.

One lady told me she was in school at Fines Creek at the time of this storm. Her dad brought a horse with quilts and blankets to get her and her sister. He wrapped them in the blankets and placed them on the horse. Her dad held to the horse's tail and walked in the horse's tracks to get through the blizzard home. Some children got no farther than the Russell home on Fines Creek, and they had to stay there for a week before the snow melted enough for them to travel.

It was a very beautiful snow. All the old timers certainly remember this one. The conditions of the snow of March 1993 were very similar.

MEMORIES OF A BEAUTIFUL, SNOWY DAY IN THE COUNTRY

We knew there had to be snow outside because there was snow on our beds, blown through the cracks in the walls of our mountain log home. Hastily we ran to the windows and there it was.

It was a cold, snowy day in the Crabtree community, way back in a cove in the Big Branch section in the early 1930s. Everything was still and beautiful. The trees and the pastures were white. The birds were still and quiet. The horses and cows were in the barn, out of the cold. The snow was still falling and except for a few dog tracks, the ground was covered with all the fluffy snow.

"My, it's a beautiful day," exclaimed Mama, putting on her boots, head scarf, and coat as she made her way to the barn to milk.

Grandma said to Grandpa, "On your way to feed the livestock, take the feed (slop) to the hogs."

Grandpa was gone for about two hours, and as he came back in the house, he carried an arm load of wood for the fireplace. Mama came back in, strained the milk, and carried it back to the spring house.

All of we girls stood looking out the window, wishing we could get out in the snow. We decided to volunteer for chores outside. We would carry in fireplace and stove wood to the porch. After much persuading, we won over.

We wrapped up with warm coats, gloves, and caps. We headed to the wood pile, stopping to throw snowballs and

Louise Nelson's Mother–Quilting on a snowy day.

even to lie down in the snow. We rolled three snowballs, put them together, and quickly made a snowman.

Like Grandpa, when we came on the porch, we had to use the broom to sweep snow off our shoes. Our fingers and toes were hurting, and our clothes were wet.

Grandma said, "Girls, take your wet shoes and coats off and hang them on the back of the chairs (cheers) to get dry."

Grandma had been busy while Mama and Grandpa were doing their chores outside. She was preparing a big dinner.

With the fire going in both the fireplace and the wood cook stove, she planned on cooking a lot. On the rod in the fireplace was placed a big black pot of back bones and ribs, and shucky beans were in the other black pot. In the oven pan she made a huge cake of corn bread. Often she put hot coals on the lid to help bake it. She later placed sweet potatoes in the stove oven and a blackberry cobbler. On the top of the stove were pots of turnips and coffee boiling.

After dinner, Grandma and Mama put up a quilt in the frames for quilting.

In the middle of the afternoon we had snow cream made from snow, milk, sugar, and vanilla. This was always a must on snowy days.

Soon it was time for Grandpa and Mama to do the outside chores. As night approached, we gathered around the fireplace, got warm, and crawled into our feather beds with warm quilts.

We really enjoyed the cold, snowy days out of school. No place could be more beautiful than the cove in the country of Big Branch. It was very pleasant being home with Grandpa, Grandma, Mama, sisters, and brothers.

MOST MEMORABLE CHRISTMAS

In the early years of the 1930s, my brother, sisters, cousins, and I could scarcely wait until Christmas morning arrived. But this year we planned to have our first Christmas tree, if at all possible.

We went to a one-room school with only one teacher for grades one through seven. This teacher was very special and she made Christmas very special. Some of the older boys and their fathers always got a big Christmas tree for the school. The children drew names and each one brought a gift for the one whose name they drew, rather than bring a gift for all of the children. One of the highlights on the season was making the decorations for the tree. The teacher got out the crayons, construction paper, and scissors. For several days they cut out balls, bells, and stars and hung them on the tree. The children popped corn and brought a needle and thread to school to string the popped corn. They each pulled their thread through the kernels with the needle until huge strings of popcorn were made. Then the tree looked beautiful. On the last day of school before the Christmas holidays, each of the children was handed a bag that had been placed under the tree for them by their beloved teacher, Miss Bessie. There would be several pieces of candy and oranges and an apple.

Our father had passed away and my mother and we children had moved into the home of our grandparents. My mother and our grandparents grew tobacco and this provided us with money for the necessary things in life. But there were no decorations for a Christmas tree.

My sister, Ruth, and I started planning to make decorations and have a Christmas tree come Christmas morning. So, on our way to the country store, we began collecting pieces of silver foil that came from cigarette packages and chewing gum packages. We used this to cover sycamore balls. Occasionally, we found a piece of gold foil. These were carefully pressed out and put in a heavy Sears and Roebuck catalog. Ruth decided to ask her teacher for scraps of construction paper. We were now making the Christmas decorations at school and saved every little scrap. We took them home and placed them in the catalog with the foil for safekeeping. These pieces of construction paper would make a beautiful loop chain for our tree.

The air was crisp and the snows had begun to fall. The Christmas spirit was greater each day. But, such disappointment—there were not enough scraps to make the chain, so we told the teacher what we were doing. She gave us several sheets of red and green construction paper to help with our project.

The tobacco had been sold so Mama, Grandma and Grandpa had some money. With the tobacco money available, Mama and Grandma were getting ready to catch a ride to town to buy presents for Christmas. They also needed bananas for the pudding and ingredients to make the chocolate cake.

Mama said, "Ruth, I believe you and Louise are old enough to stay by yourselves." Her plans were to take the three smaller children with them. "You girls feed the chickens, gather the eggs, and bring in the water and wood for the night. Grandpa will be working around the barn, if you need him. Now don't get into anything while we are away."

We had no intention of getting into anything. Our plans were to get a Christmas tree and decorate it. As soon as Mama and Grandma were out of sight, we were ready to go for the tree.

We had to make a big decision—to take the ax or the butcher knife. The butcher knife was chosen, so we carried it very carefully to the pine thicket.

We searched for a tree with a nice shape among the white pines since those were the only pine trees out there. We chose one but weren't satisfied because it wasn't really full, although it was the prettiest one we could find.

We cut first one way and then the other. Ruth took her turn and then it was my turn. After a few cuts the knife slipped and cut Ruth's finger really bad! The blood was pouring. Ruth took off her toboggan and wrapped it around the wound. We had no idea how to stop the bleeding. I grabbed up the knife and finished cutting the tree and we ran home.

Ruth had heard that if you put chimney soot on a cut it would stop the bleeding. We filled the wound full of soot which did stop the bleeding. Then we tried to clean it up with Vaseline and tied a white cloth around it, using a string from the cloth to secure the cloth on the wound. This enabled Ruth to help with decorations. She popped the corn. I strung some with the thread and needle to make a chain. It was a very slow job. We put it aside and decided to put the strips of paper together for the chain. We made a paste by mixing together flour and water. Then to secure the sycamore balls to the tree, we sewed several threads through the tops of the covered balls. Next we threaded more popcorn strings. We made paper balls, bells, and stars with tablet paper colored with crayons.

The tree wasn't cut straight, but we were afraid to try the knife again. So, we nailed the tree to two planks. It sat up sideways. After putting all the decorations on, we just sat back and admired the tree. To us it was beautiful.

We were still worried about Ruth's finger so we redressed it. Time was running out. We hurried to get the chores done. and did everything we were supposed to do. We wanted Mama to be pleased when she returned.

We found six eggs which would be enough for the banana pudding and the chocolate cake.

Mama and Grandma and the small children were all very tired when they arrived. They were loaded with presents and the ingredients to make the dinner festival.

We told Mama we had done the chores, showed them the

beautiful Christmas tree, and then told her the bad news about Ruth's finger.

The younger children liked the tree. It was hard to keep hands off of it, but they did. They had been instructed that if it fell they wouldn't have a Christmas tree.

Christmas came in two days. Ruth and I had a twenty-five cent necklace, jack rocks, and a checker board. The smaller girls had a doll and our brother got a ball and a small truck. Of course, we had a bag of oranges, apples, candy, nuts, crayons, paper, and pencils to share. There were also much-needed shoes, socks, and coats.

It was the best Christmas ever and the most beautiful sideways Christmas tree. Ruth's finger did heal.

CHAIN GANG

I lived back in the days when the covered work trucks rolled into the country roads. The trucks would stop, and out would come a bunch of men wearing white and black striped clothes.

The men wore those clothes because they could be identified by them. They were prisoners in the local prison. Some also wore chains on their legs, which is why they were called a "chain gang."

The guard with the gun stood watch as the prisoners came off the truck. His eyes were never off the prisoners.

They removed the cover from the truck bed and took out the benches. The benches were down each side inside the truck. Then they removed the picks, axes, saws, and other tools used for cleaning the road banks and repairing the roads.

Another truck would stop at a convenient place and in it would be utensils and food for cooking dinner for the prisoners. As a child, I assumed the cook was a trustworthy prisoner and didn't need guarding. I would watch the cook stack up rocks down two sides and put a metal rack on them. Then he would build a fire under the rack and put huge pots of food on to cook. The tin plates and cups were removed. At noon time the prisoners came to eat.

This work was the way the prisoners paid for their wrong doings.

Recently, a lady told me that in the days before the trucks, horses were used to pull the heavy loads. Bulldozers pulled the road scrapers. The road work was very hard, with the weather extremely hot or extremely cold.

I felt sorry for the prisoners and wondered why they did wrong. To me the road work seemed harsh punishment.

We children were afraid of the men in the work crews. Sometimes some of them escaped. Then the blood hounds were brought to search for them.

When we were on our way to the country store and saw the dogs, we would turn around and run home.

When the road was finished it was always in good condition. The community was so proud of their roads.

For the hard work and good road conditions, there was one consolation for the members of the work crews; the women in the community would cook and carry dinner to the road gang upon completion of their project.

FROM DAYS GONE BY

BRINGING THE COWS IN AT MILKING TIME
  In the early mornings of May when we went for the milk cows, we would find the pasture all frosty and we would be barefooted. Since my mother milked early, the cows would be lying down with frost on their backs. We took the opportunity of standing in the spot where the cow had lain to warm our feet.

  Most of the time we enjoyed bringing the cows in at milking time. We would play along or try to identify flowers and trees.

  One evening still quite early, our mother decided it would be best to go on for the cows. It looked very much like a terrible thunder and lightning storm was coming up. We went all over the pasture and could see them at the top of a hill a long way off.

  The storm started. We could not get the cows to start off the mountain. They were close to the barbed wire fence and the lightning was running on the lines. We were very frightened.

  After beating on the cows we eventually got them started, which seemed to take forever. The lightning and thundering was as bad as it could be. We did not have on a raincoat. In fact, I don't think we owned a raincoat. The water ran off our hair and clothes. The

A crank butter churn and a wooden
churn with a ladder back chair.

cows stayed near the fence line all the way down the mountain.

By the time we arrived at the barn we were crying and very frightened. Our mother was waiting for us at the milking shed. We were really shivering, mostly from fright. Mother tried to dry us off. She put her sweater around one of us and her apron around the other.

After the cows were milked, the storm continued, and we had to remain at the barn for a good while.

Our little twin calves didn't excite us that day. They were named Winkin and Blinkin.

CHURNING

After the milk was strained, it was taken to the springhouse and placed in the trough of water to keep cold and fresh.

By the time we were ready to drink the milk, the cream had risen to the top of the bucket. The cream was removed and placed in a crock jar to clabber. If all the cream was removed, the milk was like the skim milk we now have. The skim milk was called "blue john."

Then the process of making the butter began. This very often was the children's chore. It was too confining, so we weren't fond of churning. Sometimes Grandma gave us a nickel to churn.

The milk was placed in the wooden churn. To make the butter we worked the dash up and down until the butter formed.

In warm weather we sat on the porch; other times indoors we placed papers on the floor to catch some of the splatterings. Mopping was a must immediately after churning.

After a while the butter came and was removed from the now buttermilk. The butter was salted and pressed into a butter mold to make a pat of butter with a raised print on top.

The butter was placed in a covered pan and the buttermilk placed in buckets and put in the springhouse.

When there was extra butter, buttermilk, and milk, if a neighbor's cow was dry, we would share our milk. Most of the time there was extra milk to feed the hogs.

This was one of the necessities of life in the early days. The chores of milking and churning were every day chores, and each one knew and did his part in having milk, butter, and buttermilk.

OUR VERY SPECIAL PLACE

Growing up in the country with our mother and grandparents gave us a chance for a lot of things.

We learned all about the farming techniques. We learned just where all our foods came from. We learned the way to preserve vegetables and fruits for winter use. We learned to share, to love, to worship God, and the importance of being a happy family, from our one-room school teacher, (mine was Mrs. Bessie McClure Evans). We learned to be good neighbors.

We worked, but we had time to be children and have a good time on the farm.

We roamed over the huge farm. We discovered a place we called Echo Hill, where we could holler and the sound came back to us. We played under rock cliffs located in the mountain behind our house. We slid down the banks in the pine thicket on cardboard boxes. But, with all these places, we discovered our very special place. Our special place was a mountain spring with cold sparkling water running into a wooden tub. The tub was located in a bed of huge rocks where we sat with our feet dangling in the cool spring water.

We children spent a lot of time sitting on the rocks on hot days. Since we had no indoor bathrooms, we used the tub of water to wash our feet before retiring home for the night.

Around the sparkling cool water was a group of bushes

The valley, or cove, in wich we had our Big Branch home.

thriving from the spring. From the tub, the creek fed a pond which was made for the ducks. The livestock enjoyed the water for drinking.

The farmers would stop by to wash the tobacco gum from their hands and arms.

This is the beautiful cove where my family grew up living with my grandparents after my father's death. My stories originated from this cove at Big Branch.

Our house was located at the base of the mountain which is now surrounded by woods. When we lived there it was cleared land around the house and to the woods. There were lots of buildings around the house, and there were woods behind the house and woods to the right that led to the Jennings McCrary home, with a trail to the pasture and home of Wilson Kirkpatrick.

The fields to the main road were full of tobacco, hay, and corn. Between our house and the main road were two huge barns and pastures for the livestock.

In the lowest part of the cove in the woody mountains behind our house was a trail that led to Hyder Mountain and to the John Haney Country Store.

The road from the main Big Branch road had a bridge that went across the Big Branch as it flowed through the entire community. The farm road ended at the last barn. There was no road to our house but, we had a well-worn trail up the hill from the barn.

This was just a portion of the 225 acres of the McCrary farm that was so beautiful.

The woods to the left led farther up into the Big Branch area. The woods were very thick with chestnut trees and plenty of squirrels.

Surprisingly, at the top of the woods, was an apple orchard owned by Hubert and Winnie Wells. They got to their orchard by coming up from Hyder Mountain Road. Everyone enjoyed the beautiful setting of the orchard and the trail leading through to the Big Branch area and also the apples.

This too became a place that we children roamed but like I said, our special place was the spring area with the sparkling mountain water running into the wooden tub nestled within the thriving bushes, among the huge rocks.

We sat there so many times and just thought how wonderful it was that God provided all the things we need in life and, to us, our favorite tub of sparkling mountain water. This had to be one of God's special places, too.

SUNDAY SUMMER DAY IN THE COUNTRY

A Sunday in the summer time began when the roosters started crowing. Everyone arose to the smell of country ham or sausage cooking and coffee brewing on the wood stove.

By the time we all washed our hands and faces in the wash pan and gathered around the big kitchen table, our mother and grandmother had a big breakfast ready. The breakfast would consist of country ham, sausage, or streaked meat with eggs, gravy, buttermilk biscuits, country butter, jelly, coffee, and milk. There were times that the hens were not laying and the ham and sausage had run out. Then there might be creamed corn, applesauce, and biscuits or fried mountain trout and grits. Lots of times there was oatmeal. Grandpa declared, "That will stick to your ribs."

We girls would start immediately washing the dishes and hanging the skillets behind the stove. We each made up our beds and hurried to get dressed for church in our Sunday slippers and best dresses. On Saturday evening we had our bath, taken in the wash tub in the kitchen, so it didn't take us long to get ready. We all brushed our teeth and hung our tooth brushes on the wall.

While we were getting ready, Grandpa was checking on the livestock and feeding the hogs, and Mama was milking the cows and killing the chickens for Sunday dinner.

Sometimes she put their heads on the chop block and cut them off or wrung their necks. Then the chickens would flop around in the grass until they died.

Grandpa would get dressed in a new or good pair of overalls and shirt or sometimes he wore a suit that the landlord had given him. It was up to Grandpa to get us to church. He would say, "It's time to go to the meeting house."

Mama had small children at home. It was hard to manage small children on the long walk to church. She and Grandma prepared a big Sunday dinner that was ready when we came home.

We walked four miles from Big Branch to Crabtree Baptist Church. Therefore, we started early. We walked through the pastures and the edge of the tobacco and corn fields.

We enjoyed the Sunday School and the church services, but we lost no time arriving home to the big Sunday dinner.

Mama and Grandma had a special Sunday dinner. The dinners might consist of fried chicken or chicken and dumplings, roast turkey, back bones and ribs or some kind of hog meat. The vegetables were fresh from the garden, such as green beans, new potatoes, tomatoes, cucumber, greens, etc. There were nearly always a cake or chocolate pies, coconut pies, banana pudding, apple stack cake, or some kind of fruit cobblers. There was always some kind of canned fruits such as peaches, strawberries, blackberries, dewberries, or apples. We had big country biscuits to go with the chicken gravy and cornbread to go with the vegetables.

The aroma that filled the kitchen was unbelievable. Grandma and Mama were good cooks.

Sunday was the day that the uncles and aunts visited for dinner, so the house was full of people. The children had to wait on the second table. As many of us as could would get on the bench behind the long table.

Next was the girls' job of washing the dishes. I must say we hurried because we were anxious to get outside to play with the cousins. We played Annie Over, Hide and Seek, playhouse, etc.

All the straight split-bottomed chairs were carried to the porch where the men and womenfolk gathered around talking and telling of the progress they had made with the crops, the garden, and the canning.

Soon you would see the men showing off the new pigs or the new calves. The women would show off the garden, the can house full of the new cans they had canned, or a bunch of new chicks or ducks.

The boys would play marbles, baseball, or horseshoes. Sometimes they would go to the creek bank to fish.

We had this special place where we went to hear our echo. We would holler, "Hello, over there," and the echo would come back to us from the side of the mountain. It was something special since our cousins didn't have this special place to hear their echo.

By five o'clock the group would gather in the kitchen to eat left over supper. Then they would be on their way home.

After a wonderful afternoon of being together with the family, we would all settle on the porch until bed time, just listening to the outdoor sounds of the bugs. We would watch the chickens go to roost in the tall trees. All the children tried to catch lightning bugs. Everyone would tell what the other families had talked about. We just sat there enjoying each other and the cool of the night.

Do you remember those wonderful days in the 1930s?

BAREFOOT DAYS

We struggled to keep our slippers together until we could go barefooted. Our slipper soles had been tacked on several times. Daddy or my uncle would get the last out and the shoe tacks and tack them on. The tacks would come through and stick in our feet. Perhaps not when we tried them on, but at school and our feet would hurt the rest of the day. Sometimes when the sole came loose and it couldn't be repaired right away, we would wear a rubber can ring around them to keep them from flopping.

This was the way of life. In the country school that we attended, we were all very poor. We were all alike, so no one made fun of us. We would become very tired of trying to keep our shoes together. We could hardly wait until the right day to start going barefooted which was May 1st. This was the day every spring that Daddy let us go barefooted, even if it was cold.

We wore slippers in the summer only on Sundays. Then they were uncomfortable. Our feet were so used to being barefooted. Before we put our patent leather slippers on we would shine them with a biscuit. The biscuit kept them soft and shiny.

Going barefooted had lots of pleasant times like dangling our feet in the wooden tub with cool sparkling water, wading the branches, walking in mud puddles, or walking on the soft, green grass.

The barefoot days. From left to right: Ethel Caldwell, Ruth Kinsland, Louise Kinsland, Beatrice Kinsland, and Mazie Kinsland. All wearing dresses handmade with the material from feed sacks

There were lots of unpleasant times also. Seems we were always stumping our toes. There were no band-aids and keeping them tied up with a cloth and string was almost impossible. We stepped on bees and got stung. We were forever stepping on glass and nails. My sister stepped on a big thorn and no one could get it out. Several weeks later it worked through the top of her foot. The very worst thing we had from going barefooted was stone bruises. There was lots of pain from these. The bottoms of our feet became tough and thick. So when we had a stone bruise they had to be opened with a razor blade. We dreaded it, but this was the only way we could get relief from the pain.

Shoes are made better now, and I never see the soles flopping on them. I also never see children anticipating the day they can go barefooted on May 1st.

MOLASSES MAKING

When I first moved to my grandparents' home on the Bill and Jennings McCrary farm at Big Branch, it was in the middle of the 1930s.

It was very interesting to watch two mules hitched up to a machine. The mules went around and around in circles, making the machine grind up the cane that was fed into it to make molasses.

The fodder had been pulled off the cane stalks. The cane stalks had been cut and piled into huge stacks. This was done before the frost came.

The farm helpers fed the stalks into the machine. Everyone had a job. The women folks cooked and carried a well-prepared feast to the workers in the field.

A few years later Jennings bought a tractor to pull the cane grinder. The grinder ground the stalks and separated the waste from the juice. The waste came out onto a sled pulled by the mules.

The green juice ran through a trough into a barrel. The juice from the barrel ran into the evaporator. As soon as it hit the hot evaporator, it started boiling. It boiled in different stages through the evaporator until it turned into thick, brown molasses.

The molasses making required several workers. The men fed the stalks into the grinder. There was someone near to put

huge logs in the furnace. On both sides of the evaporator were people stirring and skimming the foam off the molasses.

The furnace was made of rocks and mud.

A molasses hoe with a long handle was used for stirring. On the last stages, skimmers were used to dip off the foam. The molasses now traveled into a huge barrel and was then placed in lard or syrup buckets.

Jennings did molasses making for other farmers for a percentage of their molasses.

Top left, friends of the Kelly's feed the cane into a motorized crusher. Bottom left, the green sap is piped into evaporators. Right, the furnace under the evaporators has to be fed constantly.

ALMOST THE SAME TECHNIQUE

I discovered Tim and Jamie Kelley were making molasses on their farm called "Chestnut Hill Farm" at Big Branch. It has been fifty-four years since I last saw molasses being made.

I also discovered that Tim and Jamie were using the same molasses machine that Jennings McCrary owned. The same machine that my grandfather, Wiley Caldwell, and my uncle, Johnny Caldwell, helped to operate in making molasses. Tim said they make approximately 150 gallons each year.

The Kelleys and their workers were using a tractor to operate the molasses machine. They used a tractor to pull away the waste from the cane stalks. This was used to feed the cattle.

The process was very much like the last time I had seen molasses made. They were using quart jars to put the molasses in instead of syrup and lard buckets. Tim said they had used the buckets for several years.

In looking out where the cane field had been, there were several rows of cane still left with the seeds in the top. I think these might be used for seeds for the next season.

Around and in the barns and sheds were several old timey machines that had been horse drawn, as well as modern equipment.

The Kelleys and his parents own the Virgil McCracken home and farm at beautiful Big Branch. They are nestled off by themselves between the rolling hills of their farm.

BOXED SUPPERS AND CAKEWALKS

The one-room school we attended was not only a place for school, but it was where the community had meetings and church services on Sunday; and it was there that I experienced my first "boxed supper."

Boxed suppers were fund raisers of sorts, where young ladies prepared a boxed, homecooked meal and it was put up for bid. The winning bidder bought the right to eat the meal with the young lady who prepared it.

We girls had gotten the right kind of candy box from the country store in preparation for the event. We covered it with red crepe paper.

The excitement had mounted up for a week as we planned what to put in our boxes. Our mother helped decide the right things for the supper. She also cooked it. We each had pieces of fried chicken, two baked sweet potatoes, two biscuits, and two pieces of chocolate pie.

We carefully carried our boxes and arrived early.

We placed our boxes on the table. Every time another box was added, ours was pushed back.

At 7:00, the auctioneer began holding up the decorated boxes and loudly asking for bids.

Boxes were selling fast. I sat rigid with fear that no one would buy mine. I wondered if it had gotten lost among the others.

I held my breath. The auctioneer was reaching for mine.

"Somebody did up a mighty pretty box here," he said. "Smells good, boys."

Then he asked, "Who will bid a dollar?" Surprisingly one guy said, "One dollar." The auctioneer got the bids up to two dollars before he decided, "Sold."

Then I became bashful, but I wasn't the only young lady to eat supper with the winning buyer. He bought two more boxes.

I carried most of my box supper home. After all, the young man ate his share out of three boxes, and all of us had food left.

We also had a cakewalk that night, where people paid ten cents each to get a chance at a cake. Several cakes and pies were given away at the cakewalks. Cakes and pies were also sold. Jars of mountain molasses and mountain honey were sold.

What simple things it took to make pleasant memories.

LYE SOAP

We moved into the home with my grandma and grandpa just as they were beginning to move out of the older ways of living.

One thing I remember was watching Grandma make lye soap. She used the ashes from the fireplace. The ashes were placed in the hopper and then boiling water was poured over the ashes to make the lye. After she had the lye ready, she then used the old lard that she had saved from cooking and a small amount of water. This was placed in the black iron wash pot outside with a fire going under it. She stirred the soap by using a long, narrow plank, being very careful that the lye soap didn't pop out on her. The soap was poured in a shallow pan and sliced into blocks.

We were cautioned not to be near the soap making.

Later the lye came in a can with a red devil on it. This was called "Red Devil Lye." Instead of using the homemade lye she started using the Red Devil.

This soap was very harsh. Everyone was careful not to get it on their body. It had many uses such as scouring the walls and floors of the old log house.

They used a long-handled broom for scouring the walls and the floor. Then they rinsed it off with boiling water. It removed the dirt as well as the grease.

The lye soap, when not in use, was stored in the loft above the kitchen.

The lye soap was a harsh working soap as would be the devil. That is why the Red Devil was placed on the can as well as the poison symbol.

We used Octagon soap for washing, bluing for keeping the white clothes white, and Lifebouy soap for baths.

MY FIRST PERMANENT WAVE

As we began to get into the teen age years, we were interested in having beautiful curly hair. Up until now, we had curled our hair with strips from brown paper bags. Then on the coffee bags was a metal strip to hold the bag together. This became a new way to curl our hair. We slept with our hair curled up in these paper or metal strips. We even tried to curl our hair by using an old fork heated in the fireplace. That didn't work.

When we heard about a permanent wave for our hair, we began picking blackberries for five cents a gallon and picking beans for fifteen cents a bushel. We saved our money. Soon we had saved $5 for the permanent wave and extra to buy material for making dresses.

My sisters and I went with the landlord to Waynesville to spend the day and to get our hair curled.

We were afraid of the electric curler that the operator would use in curling our hair. Electricity was still so new that we didn't understand what could happen with the curling machine. We talked about it for several days and hoped there wouldn't be an electric storm while we were connected to the curler.

The curling machine had lots of clamps, each with an electric cord and each clamp was connected to each curl of hair. The clamps were very heavy and it felt like our head was weighted down.

The beauty parlor operator put the curling solution on our hair then aluminum pads and then the curling clamps to each curl and turned the electricity on.

I must admit, we were very frightened.

Soon we could smell our hair burning and the operator

Mazie Gerringer, my sister, attached to an early permanent wave machine.

would be standing there fanning our head to keep down some of the burning. When the time came to turn off the electricity, we were happy young girls.

They then curled our hair on the old time curlers and combed our beautiful curls. I must say we looked beautiful.

. We then bought some bobbi pins, and we were shown how to curl our hair each time we washed it. We didn't have to curl it every night as before.

After awhile, our hair needed to be cut and we needed more permanents. We always saved out money, and no matter how scared we were of the electrical technique of getting the curls, we looked forward to getting new permanents.

The electric curling machine is the property of the Enchanted Beauty Shop in Canton, NC. They also have on display the old curler, combs, curling irons and scissors.

The curling machine originally belonged to Mrs. James Campbell. Mrs. Campbell had her beauty shop in Canton. It was in with a barber shop.

ETHEL, OUR BELOVED NEIGHBOR

Ethel was one of our favorite neighbors. Her home place is still standing, and we visit with her often to see her home and drive through the beautiful Big Branch area.

She and her husband, Claymer, built their home. Her home was so very clean and we enjoyed visiting with her. She put an apron around our shoulders, and we sat out under the shade trees while she gave each of us a hair cut.

From her springhouse, they ran a pipe with the cool spring water running through it by the side of the road near their home. Everyone enjoyed drinking from the pipe, cupping up their hands to make a cup for drinking the spring water.

She had no children, but she enjoyed all children. See the following chapter for the story she told me when she was 100 years old about keeping little Jack Caldwell for a while.

Ethel was always doing things for her neighbors. See the story that she told me about making the impressions for Mandy's teeth. (on page 105)

Today, as I am writing this section, February 19, 1996, it is Ethel's birthday and she is now 102 years old.

Ethel lives at the Brian Center, a retirement and rest home, and she just delights in doing what she can for the patients. Things like washing or combing their hair or

Mrs. Ethel McCracken, at age 102, our beloved Big Branch Neighbor
and her nephew, Mark Palmer.

brushing their teeth. You may see her pushing the wheel-
chair of a patient who is younger than she is.

It's unbelievable how sharp her memory has remained
and how beautiful she still is.

Ethel was a kind, sweet neighbor at Big Branch.

OUR LITTLE BOY FOR A SHORT TIME — Mrs. Ethel McCracken

Claymer and I lived down on Big Branch. We didn't have neighbors close to us. We had no children of our own and we thought we would love to have a child. We had both been brought up in homes with brothers and sisters.

At this time, they had children over in the County Home and we heard that all you had to do was to go over and pick out the one you wanted.

We decided that was what we wanted to do. They brought the little children out and they all looked so sad and pitiful. We saw a little boy named Jack, and Claymer knew about him and his family. So we chose Jack.

The County Home had treated the children for lice, but apparently they hadn't killed the nits in Jack's hair.

I started right away teaching Jack to do chores in the house, and Claymer was teaching him chores outside.

We were doing the dishes and Jack was drying them. He began to scratch his head and I said, "Jack, you mustn't handle your hair while you do dishes. Son, you must keep your hands clean."

When we got through with the dishes, I took him on the porch in the sunshine and looked at his head. He had a good crop of lice crawling everywhere. No wonder he couldn't keep from scratching.

When Claymer came in that night, I told him about Jack

having the lice. He took the hair clippers and he and Jack went up in the woods away from the house. Claymer cut every hair off that child's head, and I think he buried the hair in the woods.

Claymer started taking Jack to church. It was a good distance from our house, so I didn't go every Sunday. Jack and Claymer went and Jack arrived home before Claymer did. He was crying and I said, "Jack, what's the matter?" He said the boys made fun of him. I said, "Jack, you stay here with me for a few Sundays until your hair grows back some."

I said, "Jack, let this be a lesson to you. Never make fun of anyone regardless of how they look. I have seen those little boys and they have had their hair cut just like that."

Jack loved to sing and so did I. We got a song book and we would sing and read our Sunday School lesson. We had a good time together.

I had mended Jack's clothes and got him some new ones. I got him some books and started him to school at Big Branch.

Jack had the flu, and I figured I had given it to him because I washed him so much.

We had kept Jack for three months when we heard that the County Home was taking tonsils out for the children that needed it done. We took Jack back to get his tonsils out. We got someone to take Jack and me to the County Home. Claymer didn't go. I had packed all of his clothes because I didn't know when he could come back. I cried all the way, knowing we would miss him.

Jack wanted a new straw hat, so we stopped in Canton and got it for him.

When I let Jack out he looked very sad. I was sad because I came home without him. I was blue and I missed Jack a lot.

When he got well from his tonsils, the County Home said we could take him back. We had decided we had better not. We thought the county could do more for him.

I have seen Jack several times since then. He's always happy to see me, and I was happy to see him.

Jack has done mighty well. He raised a good family and sent his children to college. He has retired from a good job. Jack is a very good Christian. I'm real proud of him.

MANDY'S TEETH — Mrs. Ethel McCracken

Well, I want to tell you a little experience I had a few years back with one of my neighbors when I was living down at Big Branch. Mandy Sanford, my good neighbor, was not living too far from me and she came down to my house one day and wanted me to help her get some false teeth. I said, "Mandy, I can't do anything for that, can I?" She said, "Yes, you can write my letters." So I said, "Well, OK." She brought a paper. I believe it was called "Home Comfort." We found the ad in there where it said you could get the teeth for $18. So we wrote for the material to make the impression.

In just a few days the material and the instructions came back. We started that day to try to make the impressions.

She had her little girl, Ruby, with her. We had to keep up with the time that the impression material stayed in her mouth. So we put Ruby in the floor with the clock to keep watch of the time for us.

I mixed up that goo or whatever it was and put it in her mouth for the upper plate. Her head shook pretty bad; she was very nervous. I had to hold her head while it hardened. I had to place one hand in her mouth to hold the impression in the correct place. It was very tight when I started to take it out. I though Ruby might have timed it wrong. I started pulling, but it didn't budge. I though, oh, I will have to take her to the dentist to get this out and they might charge me

105

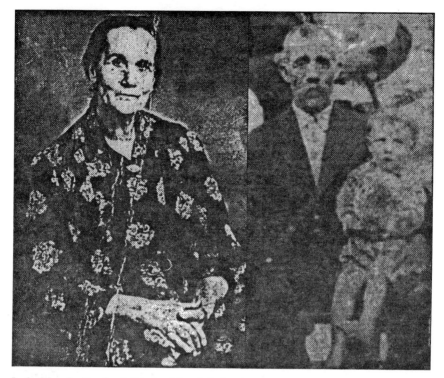

Left, Mandy Sanford. Right, Mandy's husband, Anderson Sanford, with one of their children.

with malpractice. I held her a little tighter. I wiggled and wiggled the impression. Finally, a little air got under there and it came loose. This job had really made me nervous and upset, but we laughed about it. We got started and packed all the things we needed to send back in the return box.

The next day we mailed it and in a few days we received the upper teeth and the material for making the impression for the lower teeth.

Then we proceeded to make the lower impression. Ruby gave us the correct time, and we did a little better job with the lower impression.

In a few days we had a complete set of teeth. I helped Mandy to get them in her mouth and they fit perfectly.

Mandy wore those teeth for years. In fact, she wore them as long as she lived.

COUNTRY ATTIRE

From my early years, late 1920s and early 1930s, Grandma, Grandpa, Mama, and Daddy's clothing is a big part of my remembrance.

My grandpa always wore a blue, long-sleeved work shirt, a pair of bibbed overalls, an overall coat, a felt hat, and work shoes. A friend gave him a suit, a white shirt, a better pair of shoes, and a hat for church. Grandpa looked great in these, but the overalls and long-sleeved shirt was Grandpa's style.

Many a time he came home muddy. Every night he stood outside the door, rolled down his overall legs and cleaned the cattle feed and dirt out before coming inside.

While he was eating lunch, he would hang his overall coat on the back of a straight chair by the fireplace to dry. Every wash day there were several overalls, shirts, and long unionsuits hanging on the clothes wire to dry.

When Grandpa would be getting the hay out of the hayloft for the cattle he would come upon a nest full of eggs, and he would carry these home in his hat. While he was grubbing and cleaning off the pasture he sometimes found a guinea's nest and brought home a hat full of eggs.

The things he would pull out of his overall pockets would be twine, nails, hammers, screw drivers, staples, and a pocket knife.

Grandpa in his everyday clothes.

At first I remember Grandma wearing her dresses long. She also had a three-quarter-length apron with a bow in the back, cotton stockings, and work slippers. When she went outside in the summer time she wore a handmade bonnet.

Her apron served many purposes. Her snuff box was in one pocket. She used the apron to bring in vegetables and apples. She carried shelled corn for the chickens. When we got oranges at Christmas time, she always brought an apron full of oranges to us in the afternoon. And when we were small, we would climb into Grandma's lap and she wrapped the apron around us until we fell asleep.

Grandma wore her hair in a bun and she had big, beautiful, brown eyes. Grandma was beautiful. As she aged, her hair was snowy white and she was still beautiful.

Her attire included a Sunday hat and a corset. The bloomers came to the knee with elastic in them to hold up the stockings.

Mama wore a shorter dress than Grandma, but she had a long, gathered apron with two pockets. She also carried her snuff box in her pocket. There was a handkerchief there as well to wipe away the children's tears. Mama

Ethel Caldwell, Mazie Kinsland, Louise Kinsland and Ruth Kinsland, showing off their dresses.

sometimes wore a bonnet, but as cold weather came she wore a scarf called a headrag.

Mama is tall and slender and has always worn her hair plaited around her head. Though her style has changed, an apron is still part of her attire.

For Sunday, both Grandma and Mama had handmade dresses with gathers and a belt worn low on the waist. In the late 1930s the low belt was out of style. Grandma and Mama made their everyday dresses out of feed and flour sacks. Their Sunday dresses were made from calico cloth. Calico cloth was ten cents a yard.

Daddy was not a farmer; he was a peddler. Instead of overalls, he wore suits, dress pants, and long-sleeved shirts with a hat or a dress bibbed cap. He had a pair of leather leggings he wore when he went out in the snow. Unfortunately, Daddy passed away when I was young, and I didn't see him go through all the changes in clothing styles.

The young girls wore dresses made from feed and flour sacks. The underwear was made from white flour sacks. In the summer they wore anklets. In the winter, there were

109

My mother Flora Kinsland in her apron and feedsack dress with Garrett Junior, and Beatrice.

sweaters, long cotton stockings, toboggans, and coats.

As the girls got older, they picked blackberries for five cents a gallon and bought material for making dresses and broomstick skirts and blouses, called waists.

The boys were dressed in straw hats, bibbed overalls, work shirts, and brogan shoes. They always had a pair of new overalls or a pair of dress pants and slippers for Sunday.

The babies, regardless if they were boys or girls, wore dresses, called aprons. The dresses were made from checked cloth; blue for boys and other colors for girls. They were open in the back with tiny buttons and handmade buttonholes.

These were the clothes worn by the average farmers and their families.

A FAVORITE FROM DAYS GONE BY—APPLES

We could hardly wait on the Early Harvest apples to be ready to eat. These were cooked with the peelings on. The really yellow ones were great for eating.

Then along came the June apple. Nothing could be better for eating.

Dried apples, apple pie, and an one hundred-year-old rolling pin made by my father, Garrett Kinsland.

111

In the summertime, there was the Old Timey Sweet apple. There was also a red sweet apple with a little bitter taste. Since these were sweet, they were great for baking and making preserves.

As the summer went along, there were Horse apples. This tart apple was good for applesauce or making jelly. All kinds of tart apples were made into applesauce, fried pies, and smoked apples.

Apple stack cakes were a favorite. The dough was sometimes made with molasses. The cakes were stacked in layers with the apple mixture between. They were much better if they sat a day to make them moist.

There were always apple cobblers, pies, and apple butter. Applesauce was a must on the table, with big country biscuits and country butter.

Sometimes the fried apple pies were made from dried apples or apple sauce.

To dry apples, the right apple had to be chosen, peeled, sliced, and placed on flour sacks in the sun until they were dried. At night fall, the apples were brought in the house and after the fog lifted in the morning, they were taken back in the sunshine.

As fall approached, there were many kinds of apples to store for winter use. The apples were stored in cellars or buried in the ground.

Some of the farmers' favorite apples were Horse apples, Old Timey Sweet apples, Early Harvest, June apple, Sheepnose, Pipin, Belflower, Buff, and York. There was an apple called Winter John. This apple was too sour to do anything with.

The community shared apples. There was the Hubert and Winnie Wells orchard in the community. The community enjoyed the apples from the Wells orchard. They not only enjoyed the apples but the beauty of the orchard. The setting for the orchard overlooked the community.

The apples were just one of the things that the farmer's wife delighted in. They were very important to them.

GRANDMA AND MAMA'S APRONS

An apron was a must for the farmer's wife. Both Grandma and Mama must have an apron on.

The aprons were made long, gathered long at the waist, with a neatly tied bow in the back. Aprons always had at least one pocket, but most of the time they had two pockets. It served many purposes, mainly to cover the dress to keep it clean.

Sometimes the apron would be changed two or three times a day. The bulge from one of the apron pockets of both Grandma and Mama's apron was a small snuff box with Burton's or Garrett's snuff. There was a clean handkerchief in one pocket to wipe away our tears.

We made regular trips to the birch tree to get stick brushes. We would break them in lengths about five or six inches. We carried our hands full and their apron pockets would be full also.

The apron was used to carry many things. If we found a hen's nest then they carefully carried the eggs home in their apron. However, if they purposely went to gather eggs they carried a basket.

Sometimes there would be shelled corn in the apron for the ducks and chickens.

If they were viewing their garden and ran across vegetables just right for cooking, they brought them home in their apron.

Flora Kinsland modeling one
of her many aprons.

When we were walking in the woods and found chestnuts, chinquapins or hazelnuts, they would carry these home in their aprons.

One thing I remember about Grandma's apron was her carrying oranges or apples to us at Christmas. We weren't allowed to waste them. They were put away each day until they were eaten up. She carried them to us in her apron when we were outisde working or playing.

One particular time I remember was getting caught in the rainstorm while bringing in the cows at milking time. Both my sister and I were wet. While we waited for mama to milk the cows, she took her sweater off and put it on one of us and on the other she put her apron around our shoulders.

Lots of times we would be sitting in Mama's or Grandma's lap and the weather would become cool, and they would cover us with their apron. Their lap was a good place for the baby in the family. The baby would find comfort covered in their apron while they nestled close for their nap.

Grandma wore her apron continually until her death. Until my mother's death at the age of eighty-eight every day there had to be a clean, freshly-ironed apron.

As we looked out from our house in the cove at Big Branch, we could see company coming at a long distance. Our house was nestled in the cove, but we could see the Big Branch road. There was no road to the house, so we could see the visitors walking up the hill. If they drove, we could hear their car coming through the pasture to our barn.

There would be plenty of time to sweep the porch or straighten up the house, but one of the main things that must be done was for Grandma and Mama to put on a clean apron.

TIME TO KILL THE HOGS

Around Christmas time when the temperature was just right, our family would kill the hogs.

The temperature had to be just right because we had no freezer or refrigerator. There was no electricity in the rural area as yet.

A scaffold had been made to hang the hogs on. The vats and the wash pots were full of boiling water. There was a big pile of wood to keep the water boiling.

After the hogs had been shot, they were hung on the scaffold to remove the hair and the insides.

At hog killing time the neighbors helped each other. They shared their meat, as well as their time.

After the preparations were done, they took the hogs down, cut them into the right portions, as for sausage, hams, middlings, streaked meat, roast, liver, tenderloin, back bones, and ribs, etc.

The hogs were placed on the shelf in the smokehouse to cut and prepare for curing. The smokehouse was used only for storing meat during the winter.

There were several days used in getting the meat ready for keeping and canning. The middlings had to be salted down. The hams had to be peppered, salted, and prepared just right for storing. Sometimes the hams were sugar cured. As the meat was being cut, certain pieces were used to render into lard. All the lean pieces and part of the shoulder were used to make sausage. Parts of the shoulder were canned.

The sausage was ground with a hand grinder, seasoned with dried red pepper, sage, salt, and pepper. The mixed sausage was made into balls. The balls were placed in bread pans and cooked in the oven. This prevented a lot of grease from popping over the stove. The sausage was then placed in jars which were half filled with lard. Then the cans were turned upside down, and the hot lard helped to seal the cans. When the sausage was opened to cook, the lard was used for making gravy.

The meat skins were rendered and the grease was placed in lard buckets. The small pieces of fat, after the lard was

An old sausage mill and cabbagechopper.

rendered, were called cracklings. The cracklings were made into shortening bread.

After the hog's head was cooked, it was used to make souse meat. To make souse meat, you used salt, red pepper, corn meal, and vinegar.

The liver was cooked and mashed, then mixed with red and black pepper, salt, and cornmeal to make livermush.

Tenderloins were fried usually the first night. The streaked meat was great for frying or for seasoning vegetables.

The middling or fat back was used to season dried beans and vegetables. The roast was baked. Back bones and ribs were stewed.

Everyone knows about country ham and red eye gravy or country ham and eggs.

If meat was cleaned, cured, and stored just right it would last until spring or early summer.

The sow had a litter of six to eight pigs. They were kept for a few weeks and what pigs weren't needed for making meat were sold.

Twice a day the hogs had to be fed. They were fed milk, table scraps, water, corn, and hog feed. Raising hogs for food was a full time job.

At hog killing time the neighbors helped each other. They shared their meat, as well as their time.

HARVEST TIME IN THE CORNFIELD

Cornfield beans had been planted in the cornfield because corn stalks served as a pole for the beans to climb on.

In August, the cornfield beans were ready to be picked, and we children helped.

We chose the early morning to pick when possible because the heat would be bad in the afternoons. By choosing the early mornings, we had to combat the fog, and our work clothes and shoes would be very wet when we returned home.

For our work clothes, we chose long-sleeved shirts because the corn blades would cut our arms. The blades were very sharp. Also, by choosing the long-sleeved shirts, our arms were protected from the dreaded packsaddle.

Packsaddles were fuzzy worms with stingers. They had a spot across their back that looked very much like a pack-saddle for a horse. They lived in the cornfields. If you have been stung by a packsaddle, you know there is no worse sting than that.

Gathering the beans was a family affair, as was the preparation for canning. There was a group of shade trees around the spring and springhouse. These trees were used often for shade trees just for sitting under. The trees became the spot for stringing and breaking beans to can. It seems the water from the flowing mountain spring helped to make the temperature a little cooler under the shade trees.

In the mornings, the cornfields were pretty. The spider webs were all over. We took time to view many different spider webs. In addition to spider webs the cornfields were full of morning glory vines entwined around the corn stalks. Morning glory is a beautiful flower. There would be several different colors. Between the morning glory blooms and the spider webs covered with fog, the cornfield was a beautiful sight.

In the afternoon after school hours, we began to pick the field peas. We picked may feed bags of peas, carrying them to the porch to be shelled. We had help in shelling the peas by having pea shellings. Peas had to be dry before we shelled them for storage, so we picked them in the afternoons. The hot afternoons seemed to attract the packsaddles.

One thing I remember when picking the peas was the ground cherries. The ground cherries grew wild on plants in the cornfield. When the hull and the cherry was yellow, they were ripe. It's hard to explain the taste of the ground cherry.

The farmers would soon be busy pulling the corn and getting it to the shed for shucking. When time permitted, fodder was pulled off the stalk and saved for the cattle. Most of the time, corn stalks were just cut and made into shocks until the farmer had time to gather the remaining corn and fodder.

The corn was shucked by having community corn shuckings. The corn shuckings were encouraged by the farmers' wives by having a dinner for all the shuckers.

The corn was stored in the corncrib for use for the livestock and for making meal for the family.

This procedure of taking care of the feed and the corn was done before silos.

There were corn mills for making meal for the farmer. I don't know if the community mills are available anywhere now. I believe farmers as well as everyone else depends on the grocery store for meal.

Near the end of the cornfields, the farmer planted pumpkins and candyroasters. They too were gathered and piled up around the cornshocks until cooler weather, then they were taken in for the winter storage.

Sometimes now you will see a few cornshocks, but they too are something of the past.

Very soon after the corn was shocked, the weather was colder, and the cornfields again became a pretty sight with the frost on the cornshocks and the pumpkins.

Cornshocks in a Haywood County field.

BUTTON, BUTTON, WHO'S GOT THE BUTTON?

Grandma had the buttons. In fact, Grandma had a sewing machine drawer full of buttons. On the mantle of our old country home was an old Squibb's Epson Salts box full of buttons.

This old Squibb's Salts box was sitting there when I was a young girl.

After my mother's death, among her possession, we found Grandma's button box. It was still full of buttons, a thimble, and a few hair pins.

This old Squibb's Epson Salts box is made of metal and on the box the manufacturing date is since 1858. The box could be around 100 years old.

On the fireboard were many things for safe keeping.

When clothes were ready to be discarded, Mama and Grandma cut every button off. When our dresses were made from feed and flour sacks we chose buttons from the sewing machine drawer or the button box.

We were entertained with the buttons by playing Jack In the Bush, How Many Licks? When you guessed how many buttons the other player had, you won them. Eventually one player had all the buttons.

We would choose larger buttons to make checkers out of. We made the checker-board out of cardboard and chose two different colors of buttons for the checkers.

The Squibb's Epson Salts box full of Grandma's buttons.

One game we played was Who's Got the Button? Then there was the game Zizzler. We used a large button with twine through the button eye and twisted the twine tight. Then we pulled the twine back and forth with the button making a zizzle sound.

We played school on the steps. The player with the button was the teacher. The teacher had the players guess which hand had the button in it and the player moved up one step, which was one grade. When he arrived to the top step, he then became the teacher.

Not only did we play with the buttons, we also made toys from Clarks and Coats wooden thread spools.

We cut notches around the bottom of the spools. A heavy rubber band was run through the spool and in one end of the spool through the rubber band was a small crayon. Through the rubber band at the other end of the spool was a wooden match stem or a small stick. The rubber band was twisted very tight. When released on the floor, it became a tractor.

We stacked the spools. We also made a scale of a playhouse dividing the floor plan into rooms, using the spools for the walls.

A foot-operated sewing machine.

A very small child had a toy by running a string through a group of spools. Then the string was tied together.

Wooden spools are very rare, especially the Clarks and Coats, as are the old buttons. Some of these remain in the old Singer Sewing Machine which has been in the family for approximately eighty years.

My mother's first sewing machine was a Betsy Ross.

The sewing machine was a necessity and was well taken care of.

As soon as the girls were old enough they were taught to thread the machine and the bobbin. Then they were taught to use the peddle. The old machine is controlled by how fast you peddle it. Young girls soon learned to make their clothes on the sewing machine.

BEFORE KLEENEX THERE WERE HANDKERCHIEFS

Handkerchiefs were a must in our lives as we grew up. Growing up on a farm, we were familiar with the red or blue handkerchief sticking out of the hip pocket of the farmer's overalls.

My grandfather was one of the farmers that you would find the handkerchief sticking out of his overall pocket. In the apron pocket of Grandma and Mama was always a fresh, clean handkerchief.

When we had change or bills of money to carry to the county store it was tied in the corner of one of their handkerchiefs. After it was secure in the corner of the handkerchief, it was pinned inside our dress with a big latch pin.

Just before we got to the store we would take the pin off the handkerchief, but we would not untie the money until we arrived in the store. We didn't want to take a chance of losing it.

Mama and Grandma secured their money in the same way when they were going to town. I remember they tied their money in the handerkchief before placing it in a leather change purse. They then placed the change purse in their pocketbook.

Treasures such as brooches or rings would be tied in the corner of a handkerchief and placed in the old pocketbook for safe keeping.

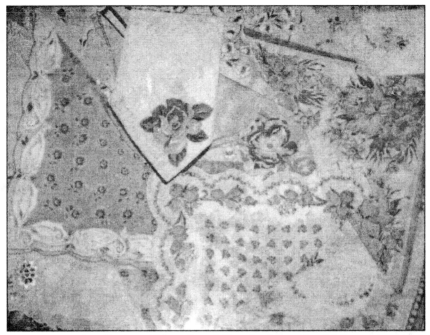

A collection of Mama's and Grandma's handkerchiefs.

There were also Sunday handerkchiefs in their dress or coat pockets. Just before we girls started off to school or church, we placed a handkerchief in our dress or coat pocket.

My niece preserved Grandma's handkerchiefs by washing, ironing, and folding them. She placed them in a frame and made a beautiful wall hanging.

My sister gathered up Mama's handkerchiefs and also made a beautiful wall hanging.

A lot of Mama's and Grandma's handkerchiefs were handmade. In the corners they embroidered flowers, birds, or butterflies. Then there were handkerchiefs with handmade tatting.

Over the years they had bought lots of handkerchiefs, but many of their handkerchiefs were presents.

Sometimes when they received letters from friends or relatives, they would receive a beautiful handkerchief bought just for them. Their olden days were survived without the luxuries of these days and Kleenex was not heard of.

CORNBREAD

What made cornbread special?

It took a lot to get a corn field ready for planting. The farmer began early in the spring with plowing and fertilizing the ground in preparation for planting.

My grandfather liked to follow the signs for planting. The time he chose to plant corn was when the dogwoods were in bloom.

The farmers cultivated each row and each row was hoed and not a weed was left in the corn field.

When the corn was grown and ready to harvest, the fodder was pulled off and the corn stalks with the corn was put into cornshocks until the time to shuck it.

The farmers had acquired a corn shucker pulled by a tractor. It didn't remove all the corn shucks. They would get together on Saturdays and have a corn shucking. The farmer's wife encouraged the corn shuckings by preparing a dinner and the children along with the grown ups enjoyed the corn shuckings.

Eventually the corn was ready to place in a corncrib, made with openings so the corn could have a lot of air.

Saturday was the time to take corn to the corn mill to be ground into meal for mush and cornbread. Friday nights the corn was brought in the house and each member shelled corn.

Only the nice ears of corn were used for meal. There was always a lot of nubbin's left for the cows, horses, and pigs.

It always helped to have a corn cob to begin shelling the ear of corn. This was a rough job on the hands.

Grandpa took the horse and the wagon with bags of shelled corn for both himself and the landlord to be ground into cornmeal.

He paid the miller a certain portion of meal for grinding the corn. When farmers ran out of meal they could buy meal from the miller.

After the meal was brought home, it was placed in the mealbox which was handmade and ideal for storage.

The bran remained in the meal and a big round sifter was in the top of the mealbox for sifting the meal.

This was long before self-rising meal, so the cook had to add soda and salt and buttermilk when mixing the cornbread.

Supper nearly always featured cornbread and milk. The farm house with a wood stove going and a big bread pan of cornbread and leftovers was the simple way for the farmer's wife to end the long day of work. It was a time of day and a meal that remains in the mind of every one that experienced it.

A cast-iron pan of cornbread and cornmeal muffins fresh from a wood stove.

FUN DOING OUR CHORES

In the fall of the year farmers had many chores, as did the children.

One of our chores was picking the black-eyed peas, shelling them, and storing them for winter use.

After school was out, we got our old clothes and shoes and went to the cornfield to pick peas. The peas had grown up the corn stalks. Our pea patch was some distance from our home. We took feed sacks to pick the peas in. The peas were very light but awkward to carry, but we always managed to get them home.

We had plans for a pea shelling as soon as the peas were picked. This encouraged us to pick and have the peas ready.

While picking on the side of the hill, we could hear the donkeys braying at the Mark Bishop home.

Mark and his wife, Beenie, who we all called aunt and uncle, lived past a patch of woods in a clearing above the pea patch.

As the donkeys brayed more, we decided when the peas were picked we would journey up the hill, past the woods, and into the clearing where the donkeys were.

As we approached the Bishop's home, Uncle Mark and Aunt Beenie were sitting on the porch. Uncle Mark had on his overalls and long-sleeved work shirt, brogans, and a straw hat. Aunt Beenie was dressed in a long dress and apron with her hair up in a bun. They were enjoying the cool of the evening.

The dogs barked at us, so we hesitated to go on. Uncle Mark convinced the dogs to return to the porch and lie down.

We told Uncle Mark our reason for the visit was that we wanted to see the donkeys and hear them bray.

He invited us to sit on the porch for a spell while he got the feed together for the animals. It was just the right time of the day to feed the animals.

He gathered up the hog and chicken feed, then got the bucket to carry the donkey's feed in. He said, "Now watch. The donkeys will bray when they see me coming with the feed." Sure enough, they did. When they opened their mouths to bray, we were amazed at such big teeth.

We had many of the same kinds of animals as Uncle Mark showed us: chickens, turkeys, hogs, cats, dogs, and mules, but we had no donkeys. I must say it was very exciting to see a donkey for the first time and hear it bray, "Hee Haw."

After several evenings, we had the peas picked and were waiting for the pea shelling.

Grandpa and Uncle Johnny had lit several lanterns and tubs on the porch were ready for the peas to be shelled. When the peas were shelled, we had the cracks in the porch full of spillage.

The older folks continued shelling, but Mama had a treat for us. She had chocolate cake and hot chocolate. Our friends enjoyed the treat, and then we were all in for playing a game of hide and seek in the dark. We gave up on finding the boys. They had chosen to hide in the barn, and we weren't brave enough to face the dark to find them.

Farmers and their families had lots of chores to do, but they had lots of fun doing them.

Saturday afternoons the boys got together to hear the fights on the radio. Then on Saturday night they got together with my Uncle Johnny to listen to the Grand Old Opry.

On Sunday afternoon the ball field in the pasture was full of friends to have a ball game. Nothing could be better than a cow pasture ball game.

We all had the same style of living on the farm and many chores to do. We all enjoyed gathering together.

MONDAY WAS WASH DAY

Every Monday morning was wash day if it wasn't raining. In the summertime the children carried water to fill the big black iron pot with a fire built under it for boiling the clothes.

The white clothes would be boiled in the wash pot with a long wooden paddle for stirring.

There was a long bench that held three galvanized tubs. These tubs were filled with water for washing and rinsing. In one tub bluing was dissolving to rinse the white clothes in.

Warm water with octagon soap was used to rub the dirt out of the clothes. The clothes were rubbed up and down on the washboard. This was long before detergents and Clorox.

Most of the clothes were made of cotton. The starch was made with water and flour boiled together. If the starch was thick, it was strained.

On Saturdays all the beds had to be changed, so we had lots of sheets made from sheeting cloth. The pillow cases (pillow slips) were all specially made. Some of them were edged with handmade tatted lace. The others all had beautiful embroidered designs. The girls of the family learned embroidering when they were very young.

During winter months the clothes were washed in the kitchen. There would be wash tubs of water heating on top of the wood cook stove and the reservoir on the side of the stove would be full of water.

The bench from the kitchen was the wash bench.

As the clothes were hung out they froze hard. If they weren't dry before night they were gathered in and hung on the back of chairs or behind the wood cook stove to finish drying.

The clothes lines were filled with white sheets blowing in the wind as soon as they could get them out. If the weather was nice the sheets could be taken in and then the other clothes remained on the lines until later in the day. With our family as large as it was, even the barbed wire fence was full.

The women folks prided themselves in having a clean wash.

IRONING DAYS

Ironing days were usually on Tuesday.

In the winter months there were several black irons sitting on the wood cook stove or heating in the fireplace.

The irons had to be held with a heavy cloth but very soon they were cold and had to be replaced in the coals to heat up again.

Most of the clothes were made from cotton, which was hard to iron. All the clothes were ironed.

Usually two people ironed at the same time. One ironed on the ironing board and the other on the work table. The girls were taught to iron early in life.

In the summer months when the beans were cooking, the irons were heated on the cook stove.

The farmer's wife had to be on schedule to get all the work done. With all the necessary jobs of a farmer's wife and the children helping in the fields by Saturday afternoon the work was done and there was time to see that the children had their baths and time to have the house clean for Sundays. There was time for the Sunday cakes to be baked.

With all the work that the farmer's wife had to do, you never found clothes piled up waiting to be ironed.

CHESTNUTS AND SQUIRRELS

Along the trail from our house to the one-room school was a woods completely covered with chestnut trees.

It was hard to walk along the trail in the fall of the year when the big burry hulls holding the chestnuts had fallen to the ground and the trail was covered.

We took buckets and baskets to the woods to gather chestnuts. My sisters and I had fun gathering chestnuts, as we did all the nuts that grew wild on the farm.

Chestnuts didn't last as long as the other nuts when gathered but while they lasted they were boiled, baked, made into dressing, or eaten raw.

While we were picking up chestnuts it was very interesting to watch the squirrels at work. They would be running all over the ground where the chestnuts were. They could tell by the weight or feel of the chestnut whether it was a good one.

We would sit on rocks and watch the many beautiful, fluffy-tailed gray squirrels gathering chestnuts. They picked up a chestnut with their front feet, and when they decided it was a good one, they put it in their mouth and scampered up the tree. When getting to the branches near the top they would jump to other branches or to other close by trees and very swiftly go to their nests.

Since all the leaves had fallen off the trees, we could see many squirrel nests. They were so busy gathering nuts they didn't seem to notice us observing them. Some of them would be close to us.

Unfortunately, this part of the woods was a favorite spot for squirrel hunters. My uncle and his friends were some of the hunters.

God had provided the squirrels for food as He did the chestnuts and the many things that grew wild in the country.

Squirrels were stewed and a gravy was made in the same pot. The family enjoyed the squirrel and gravy with home-made biscuits.

Chestnut trees took a blight, and all the trees were killed. There are very few chestnut trees growing wild now.

FARM COUNTRY WAS A FAVORITE PLACE TO PLAY

Children weren't supposed to work all the time in the farm country. There was plenty of time to play.

Living on a large farm, which consisted of meadows, hills, coves, branches, mountain springs, woods, and small mountains gave us a variety of places to roam around and play.

In the Big Branch area where we lived on the farm of approximately 225 acres with our mother and grandparents, we had plenty of room to explore.

Big Branch was named for the big branch that ran through the entire community. The branch began as streams running from the many coves in the Big Branch area. The streams ran to the valley in the lowest level of the community. As it went along, it picked up more and more small branches that ran from the mountain springs and it became a big branch by the time it went through the community and into the Pigeon river, then on into Tennessee.

I mentioned the big branch because it was a favorite place to play throughout the community.

We waded in the branch on the slick rocks, and if we fell it didn't matter for soon we were wet anyway. Some of the children tried their luck at swimming.

On the side of the branch was plenty of sand and rocks, where girls spent a lots of hours making playhouses.

The boys of the community used the branch banks to trap

Hides were a sorce of income for many of the country boys.

for muskrats, so they could sell their hides.

The meadows consisted of low farming country. The children worked and played around the crops in the meadows. The meadows became a favorite place for the Sunday afternoon baseball games. These places were called "the bottoms."

The hilly areas were also used for farming. They were good places to take the beagle dogs and rabbit hunt.

Blackberries, huckleberries, strawberries, and dewberries grew on the hilly areas. The children spent a lot of time with the parents picking berries, but they also went there just to pick and eat the wild berries.

Among the bushy areas were chinquapins, hickory nuts, chestnuts, black and white walnuts, and hazelnuts. It was fun picking all these nuts.

We enjoyed sitting and watching the squirrels gather nuts. Our cousins really enjoyed the Sunday afternoons with us in the hills where the nuts and squirrels were.

On the hill just beyond our house was a pine thicket. In the pine thicket was a huge gully that picked up the overflow of water after a heavy rainfall. Other times the gully was dry. We children cleaned up the gully for a purpose. The purpose was to have a landing place for our cardboard box that we used to slide down the hill slick with pine needles. The pine needles were so slick we had to go back through the edge of the pine trees to get to the top to start our sliding.

There were many huge grape vines growing in the hollow below our house. These grape vines became swings. They had to be tested first to see if they would hold us before we could swing on them.

Back in one of the mountains, covered with trees, was a rock cliff. It was steep and rough to the top of the cliff. We didn't try to climb to the top, but underneath the cliff was a trail from the farm to the neighbor's farm. We played under the shelter of this cliff. If there were spiders and snakes there, we didn't see them.

A neighbor had an apple orchard at the top of one of the steep hills joining the farm where we lived. After the climb to the top of the hill, the land became flatter and there was the apple orchard.

In the orchard was a group of flat rocks. That became our picnic spot. The woods surrounded the orchard and we couldn't see beyond that, but it was a very enjoyable place.

Traveling over the hilly pastures to bring the cows in for milking was not a bad job because we played along as we went for them. We would go from pasture to pasture going across the stile that was built across the barbed wire or the rock fence leading us to the pasture where we could hear the cow bells and bring the cows in for milking.

We had a habit of gathering wild flowers and trying to identify them. We always found different ones on the trips for the cows.

We played all over the farm, but we had a very favorite spot where the water flowed from the mountain spring into a wooden tub. Nestled around the tub was a group of rocks where we sat with our feet dangling in the cool mountain water.

Not only did we take advantage of the farm for entertainment, we also used sticks and other things we found on the farm for making toys like whistles, stilts, sling shots, and pop guns.

Among the many games played by the children were hopscotch, hide and seek, annie over, marbles, walking stilts, can lid rolling, and many others that required no money to buy.

There were many inside games because there was no television. There was a battery radio. Books were scarce. A lot of the games were played with handmade toys.

We had a few games the whole family owned such as Old Maid cards, checkers, jack rocks, and Chinese checkers.

Life was beautiful for children living on the farm. I'm happy I was one of the children that was fortunate to have the privilege.

GUINEAS

Guineas are beautiful. They are dark gray, speckled with white spots. They have a ridge on top of their heads and they look much like pheasants. I believe they are originally from Guinea.

Guineas are very hard to raise due to the fact they like to roam in the field away from the house and barn. They came near the barn where feed was left out for them, but they came when no one was near the barn.

There was no way you could get them into the chicken house to roost. They found security in roosting in the branches of the tall trees.

Guineas were very noisy fowl. If an animal or person approached them, they let the world know they were around. Their noisy sound was very quarrelsome. In fact, they made good watch dogs.

Grandma loved raising guineas. She had her own way of hatching the small, speckled eggs.

She loved to have an assortment of different chickens, like the ones with the long feathers and the ones with a top-knot head. Since the guineas were different they were special to her.

The guineas chose to lay their eggs away from the house. All the guineas laid eggs in the same nest. They made their nest in the broom sage or in the bushy area of the pastures. Their laying time was between 12 p.m. and 2 p.m.

We girls would go to the spot where we could hear the guineas cackling. We would go early before they started laying eggs and we would wait until they left the area where the nest was. Grandma told us to take the long handled galvanized spoons but to be careful that we touched only the handle. She said they were like birds, if they knew their nest had been tampered with they would leave it.

A guinea

We would find a basket full of eggs. We always left about half of them so the guineas would continue laying in the same nest.

Grandma would catch hens setting and she placed the eggs under the hens to hatch. Soon she would have dozens of baby guineas. She delighted in giving the baby guineas to her neighbors so they could have guineas on their farm.

The guineas were somewhat like the mother hen. She could cluck to her babies. You could see broods of baby guineas following the mother guineas in the field.

Some of the guineas would get killed by wild animals or dogs, but there was always a tree full of guineas come roosting time.

A few times we had guinea stew with gravy, but the family didn't like the taste.

Just recently a lady called to tell me that she got her first bunch of baby guineas from the ones that Grandma's hens had hatched.

They are rare around farms now. The yards used to be full of hens, baby chicks, and roosters, and the ponds and surrounding areas were full of ducks, but guineas had their place in the field.

A GOOD SHEPHERD

Back in the late 1920s and 1930s farmers had herds of sheep on their farms.

A good farmer loved his sheep; therefore, they became good shepherds. A good shepherd took care of his sheep.

On the farm where my grandfather lived, he and the landlord led the sheep to the high pasture in the summertime.

All fences were made with many strands of barbed wire to keep the sheep in the pasture. However, they sometimes wandered away and had to be herded back to their fold.

In the farmer's yard was a bell that was rung only if an emergency arrived. If the bell rang, the farmers returned to the house.

At times when the farmer's wife could hear the sheep bleating and their bells ringing, she would know there was trouble. She could hear the dogs barking, also. At this time she rang the bell for the farmer's alert.

The farmers would go immediately to the pasture to find stray dogs among the sheep. Very often, several of the sheep would be killed by stray dogs.

Sheep are so humble when a dog attacks them they would just give in to them.

Sheep have no sense of direction. Like the shepherds in the Bible who watched the sheep, they used a crooked rod to pull the sheep out of the bushes and from high cliffs, getting them back to their fold.

In the winter months sheep were kept in a pasture around the barns. The farmers fed them grain and hay.

In March of 1936, the pastures were getting green, and my grandfather and the landlord had turned the sheep to the high pastures.

A surprisingly deep snow came. My grandfather and the landlord made their way to the hilly pasture in search of the sheep because they had no food. They had no sense of direction and had not returned to the barn.

When they reached the sheep on this snowy day, they started rolling a snowball down the steep, hilly pasture. As it rolled down the pasture to make a path for the sheep, it became very large. When the snowball came to a halt, it landed behind the barn on the north side where the sun had no strength at that time of year. This huge snowball took nearly two months to melt.

Being good shepherds, my grandfather and the landlord led the sheep down the trail to the barn to feed them where they remained until the late snow melted.

In the spring time the pastures would be full of white, fluffy lambs jumping and frolicking. It was a beautiful sight. It was also a pleasant sound, listening to the baa-ing and the many bells ringing.

The farmers gained income from the sheep's wool. Down in the corral from the pasture to the barn, the sheep flocked together waiting for their wool to be sheared off. One by one they were sheared and put back into the pasture. There were bags and bags of sheep wool to be sold to make clothes.

There were extra lambs growing into sheep, so the older ones were sold for mutton. When the sheep were one year old, they began having lambs.

The landlord roasted sheep in the yard on a rod where they were turned often and where the wood fire was just right for roasting.

By the side of my grandmother's bed were sheep skins with soft, fleecy wool. She kept those sheep wools washed and brushed. The skins were very warm when getting out of bed on the cold, wintry mornings.

The sheep wools were used in sick beds to prevent bed sores.

My grandmother and mother used the sheep wool to put between the quilt tops and the flannel linings to make warm quilts.

Those are some of the ways the farmers and their wives took advantage of things from the farm to make their living better.

Being a good shepherd was not hard for my grandfather or the landlord because they loved raising sheep.

On Sunday afternoons when my grandfather wasn't busy doing the farm work you could see him in the pasture checking on the sheep.

PATTERN FOR LIFE

My life as a young girl was simple. Life was full of drudgery. We were very poor.

After my father's death when I was ten years old, we moved into the home with my grandparents, uncles, and cousins. They lived as tenant farmers. The house was cold and very crowded. Those were the days of no electricity, so there were no conveniences in the home. Nearly everyone in the community lived as we did.

My pattern for life—Lucille McCrary with Sam and Katherine McCrary

Even though we were poor, we had enough food, and my mother and grandmother were good cooks.

Clothes were a different phase of life. We had hand-me-down clothes. There were two good dresses for school and one for church. Those were made from feed or flour sacks and store bought material with the money we girls received from picking blackberries for five cents a gallon. Our underclothes were made from white flour sacks. We had a pair of Sunday shoes and when they were very worn, they became school shoes. We had one pair in the early spring for Sunday and another pair at Christmas, bought with tobacco money. Summertime we went barefoot.

By the time I was eleven years old I met a special friend, Katherine McCrary. I visited her a lot. Katherine's clothing were so pretty and neat. I admired them. Katherine didn't let my being poor bother her. We remained the best of friends. While I was with Katherine at her home, I found the pattern for my life. My pattern was Katherine's mother, Lucille. She was so neat and clean, and I felt she really had an interest in me. She was a great cook. Sunday afternoons while Katherine and I played on the banks of the big branch with rocks and sand, her mother invited us in for cake and milk.

The cooking didn't compare with what a special person Lucille was. She was a good Christian, a good person all the way around.

Oh, how I admired the person she was. I kept telling myself, "when I grow up, I want to be like Lucille."

Sunday mornings we went to Crabtree Baptist Church with our grandfather. We walked the four miles there and back. Sunday nights, Lucille invited us to go to Hyder Mountain (Finchers Chapel) with her and her family. She talked to me about letting God be a big part of my life. I felt special. She loved me and she showed it.

During a revival, Katherine, my sisters, and I were sitting together in church. That night I went down the aisle and gave my heart to God. Immediately, my pattern in life was by my side. She said, "Louise, I'm proud of you. Always do right and let God be your leader."

As years went by and I had my own home, I tried out the things I learned from my pattern. I tried to be friends to other people. I thought about Lucille's clean house and tried to keep my house like she had. The most important part of my pattern came through living a Christian life as best I could. I've been teaching the first grade Sunday School department for forty years which is one way I can express what being a Christian means to me. There have been times in my life I would think of Lucille when I was making a decision between right and wrong. I often remember her ways of life.

I hope we too can be a pattern for someone. I hope we will live our lives so others will want to follow us.

HORSE DRAWN AND OLD FARM EQUIPMENT AND HAND POWERED TOOLS

For a few years, I've been collecting pictures of old horse drawn farm equipment and hand-powered tools.

I can't identify all of them. My cousin, Jack Caldwell, has taken me to several barns where we got some pictures. Jack could identify all of them, but unfortunately Jack passed away before we could finish our project.

When my family moved into my grandfather's house, he was still using some of the old equipment. Little by little there were gradual changes in equipment and tools.

I remember the mules pulling the old molasses mill around

A horse drawn wagon.

Frank H. Haynes cutting hay over fifty years ago on Chambers Mt. with a horse drawn hay cutter.

to grind up the cane and using the old boiler to boil the syrup.

The horses were still pulling the hay cutter and the hay rack was used. The hay was also stacked into hay stacks at the end of the barn, and the hayloft was used to store hay.

Grandpa was still plowing with the mules and used some of these different implements: the harrow, the cultivator, the fertilizer, corn planter, and many others.

The tobacco was being cut with tobacco cutters and hung in the barn loft. There were wheat cradles, sickle blades, and mowing blades.

The corn was cut and shocked and tied with grass strings. Later there was a corn shucker, a corn chopper, and a silo for storing chopped-up corn stalks.

There were hand-held sheep shears.

Gradually you could see the hay wagon and the sled put aside for the tractor.

All the wood was cut with cross cut saws, chopped with axes, and hauled to the wood shed by mules pulling the sled.

The handmade shingles for the roof were made by the farmers with hand tools.

Some of the old tools were poleax, mallet, wedge, go-devil, auger, maul, froe, crowbar, drawing knife, and peavy.

A double foot plow.

There was an old horse drawn buggy stored in the barn on the farm where we lived.

Some of the pictures I have collected are of equipment older than the ones used when I lived on the farm.

While reminiscing with Jack about the old plows he told me this story:

"My family was very poor. My brother, two sisters, and I lived alone with our mother. We had no means of making a living. My mother helped out on the farm where I lived. She worked in the field like a man would.

"My cousin, Glenn, came to visit us and it was springtime. My mother wanted to get the garden plowed so she could get it started growing. In the summertime that was where our food came from. My brother, Wiley, and I decided we would pull the plow through the garden if Glenn would push it. The ground was pretty loose. We pushed and pulled the plow until we had it pretty well cut up. Then we took rakes and raked it out. My mother planted her garden that day."

LIFE AND TESTIMONY OF JACK CALDWELL

(This story is typical of the very poor families. Jack is my cousin and has given me permission to add this to my book.)

During the depression, we lived at the head of Big Branch in Penland Cove. I think I was about six or seven.

Rufe Penland owned the 100-acre cove.

There were me, mother, my cousin, Annie, Wiley, Connie, Lillie Mae, Lee, and Glenn Keener and his mother. We all lived in the tenant houses.

I remember we lived in a little old log house that had a loft. I always like to sleep in the loft.

Times were really hard with the depression on.

I was just a little kid, but I remember, Glenn and my brother Wiley going out and killing squirrels and birds and bringing them in for us to eat to keep from starving to death. We didn't have much to eat. We got down to eating cornbread and water. We'd go out to the spring and bring in the cold water and crumble the cold cornbread in it.

Times were so hard and my mother had no one to help her except us kids. She would catch a ride to Waynesville or walk and get food for us from the welfare.

I remember the first day I went to school. Miss Bessie McClure was my teacher. She put me on a seat and I got to rolling back and forth making noises. She then put me on an old homemade bench and I couldn't make a noise on that.

Jack and Myrtle Caldwell, 1995

I remember the old pot-bellied stove. We put our cornbread and milk in the water under a big tree to keep it cool. We carried it to school in a pint jar with our spoon down in it.

I went to school one morning and Miss Bessie looked down at my feet. She said, "Jack, your feet are dirty. Go out to the branch and wash them." I found the sandiest spot I could find. I rubbed sand over my feet until I got them clean. This was the way I cleaned them at home because we had no soap.

I also remember Miss Bessie bought me the first pair of overalls that I ever had.

I also remember the first pair of shoes that I owned. They were rough, brogan shoes. I had a hard time learning to walk in them.

When I went for the cows on frosty mornings, I would be barefooted. I would stick my feet in the branch to get them warm and to keep them from getting frostbitten.

Times were harder every day.

Mr. Jennings McCrary came and took us to the County Home. The County Home was a place where they put people that weren't able to provide for themselves. The county fed and clothed them.

At this time by brother Wiley had gone to stay with Rastus Green in Clyde. My sister Connie had gone to stay with Lillie Stockman in Beaverdam. That just left me, Lillie Mae, and Mother.

When we pulled up to the County Home, I began to cry and said, "I want to go home." No matter how poor it was, home was home.

I was eight years old.

They told me there was a big bunch of children there and I would always have someone to play with. They finally got me out of the car. I went in and after a while I got adjusted to it.

At the County Home they had a huge farm. We made lots of corn, tobacco, and large gardens. There was a large bunch of hogs and chickens to take care of. We did a lot of work. We made up to fourteen hundred bushels of corn. I don't know how much wheat we made. We had a big dairy and had our own milk and butter. We had chickens and eggs to eat. We were just about a self-supporting place. We worked hard.

My mother and my sister Lillie Mae left to live with some people and that left me there by myself. They said they didn't want me. I didn't see my mother again for four years.

Then people started coming and getting me to live with them. From the time I was eight years old until I was eleven years I stayed in eleven different homes. I never did know what a real home was. I was just everywhere. I missed my mother and my family. I kept longing for the day I would see them.

I finally found out where my mother was and I left the County Home to be with her. Someone had told her that she could get work in Florida. So we set out hitch hiking. When we got there we were raggedy and dirty from riding in box cars. We were starved. We got into a section that had rich people. They gave us some money and food.

We messed around in town for a while and mother decided she couldn't get any work. So she decided that we would go back home. We set out walking from Jacksonville, Florida, to Clyde, North Carolina. I don't know how many barns we slept in on our way home. We would stop at homes and beg for food. One night we came to a big pine thicket and we spent the night there. Along in the night I told my mother,

"I'm freezing." She pulled her apron off and put it around me.

We were going along the road the next morning and thumbing. A fellow stopped and asked us where we were going. We told him we were going to Clyde, North Carolina. He said, "That's where I am going." So, he brought us into Clyde.

Mama said, "Let's go to Aunt Dollie's and Uncle Wiley's." She knew the way. We were going across the mountain from Clyde to Big Branch. On the way it got dark. There was an old log barn. We lay down in the barn and went to sleep. The next morning we ate raw roasting ears for breakfast from a big corn field.

I guess all in all I had one of the worst times that could be had. I've had a hard road but I'm still here. Thank the Lord.

This is how I came to know the Lord. I was living at Wilson Kirkpatrick's at this time. He lived at Hyder Mountain. My mother, Lillie Mae, and I moved there to help him run the farm. He also had a dairy barn.

I met a fellow by the name of Gilbert Jolley. He asked me to go to church with him. I never knew a preacher, never seen a Bible, and never heard a prayer prayed. I never knew anything about the Lord. As I heard people talking about the Lord, I began to have a fear of the Lord. I was seventeen at this time.

I went to church with Gilbert Jolley that night and the Lord got hold of me. I didn't sleep good that night. I was under conviction.

The next day when I was hoeing corn, my mind was still bothered. I told the Lord if you will let me get back to church tonight, I will give you my heart. At the end of the day I thought about what I had promised the Lord. I went to church and sat in the very back.

Mr. Dock Russell and Jarvis Teague were the preachers at this revival at Antioch Church. I was under conviction all during the service and that night I gave my heart to the Lord. This was May, 1943. This was the turning point in my life.

I left Wilson Kirkpatrick's and went into the Navy on May 6, 1944. I was discharged February 6, 1946.

I went to farming in Ironduff. Then I went to the CC Camp in Robbinsville. I was working on VA training. I made thirty dollars a month, and I sent my mother twenty six dollars of this each month.

When I came back, my mother and I lived across the river on Fulbright's place. Then I went to work at Wellco.

This is when I met Myrtle. She was baby-sitting at the home of Lawrence and Sarah Parker.

Then Myrtle moved to Asheville to work. I had a friend get her address for me. I wrote to Myrtle and she answered my letter. I asked the Lord, "If it's your will, let me and Myrtle get together." Thank God he did.

I helped build the house that we are living in now. Myrtle and I got married right in front of the window in the living room.

Our first baby, Emily, was born when we lived across the river in Ironduff. We moved to the Chambers place and Leon was born there.

The house came up for sale and we bought it and my mother moved in with us.

Mother and I were getting out wood. We came home and mother got sick. Myrtle helped her get dressed. We got her in the truck and when we got to the emergency room, Myrtle ran in to get some help. Mother fell over on my shoulder and died.

My children got through school and college and both have good spouses and good jobs.

I retired from Wellco after thirty-four years.

We still live in the little house that I helped to build, then rented, and then bought.

I've been teaching Sunday School and have been active in church and am now a deacon. This is what my life has been like for the past years. I'm in my fortieth year of marriage to Myrtle. This is the finest thing that happened to me, when I met and married Myrtle Metcalf.

If it had not been for the Lord and his guiding me through all the years of struggle, I could not have made it.

I thank God for everything.

COULD YOU BELIEVE THIS? MYSTERIES OF JAKE

On November 21, 1886, John (Jake) Justice was born to Jim and Lizzie Price Justice. The Justice's had three other children besides Jake: Henry, Tommy, and Dollie. They lived in the Fines Creek area of Haywood County.

At the youthful age of fifteen, Jake's mother sold him to John Green and his wife for $100. The agreement was to bring him back home in one year. This was 1901.

Jake's mother, hating to see him go, followed the Greens and their wagon to Bear Wallow Gap. When she told him she would see him at the end of the term, he said, "Mom, you won't ever see me again." Jake was very sad.

The Greens and Jake had a loaded wagon with four horses. They traveled approximately fifteen miles a day. The journey was fifty miles and they made the trip in four days. They traveled through Bear Wallow Gap and Del Rio, Tennessee, to Sevierville, Tennessee.

Whether or not the Tennessee farm was already purchased is not known.

Jake worked in the fields but his heart was with his homefolks. However, he learned much from Mr. Green.

When Jake was twenty-five years old he married Sarah Clifton. The had three children: Paul, Esco, and Glover.

Jake got a job with the Tennessee Steamboat Company as a deck hand. The steamboat was the means of moving lumber and other supplies from Knoxville to Dandridge, Tennessee.

He picked up a magazine or newspaper and saw a story

Jake Justice, Dollie Justice, and Tommy Justice. This picture was taken after Grandma, Uncle Jake and Uncle Tommy were reunited. They were always telling us stories, but this one was so hard to believe.

about a woman doing quilting. The woman was Dollie Justice Caldwell from Haywood County, North Carolina. He knew this must be his sister. So he and his son made plans to go back to Haywood County in search of his family. This was thrity-five years later.

He arrived in the Crabtree area and found where his brother Tommy lived. He hold him he was traveling and needed a place to spend the night. Tommy invited him in. Then Jake told him he was his brother. They were excited about seeing each other again after so many years.

Tommy and Jake made plans to visit their sister, Dollie, the next day. She lived in the Big Branch area.

Tommy and Jake found Wiley, Dollie's husband, grubbing on a creek bank. Wiley walked to the house with them. When arriving at Dollie's house, Tommy announced, "This is our brother." Dollie replied, "My brothers Jake and Henry are both dead." Jake said, "I'm Jake and I'm very much alive." The three rejoiced over getting to know each other again. There was lots of catching up to do.

After this, Jake caught the Trailways bus to Waynesville and hitchhiked to Crabtree and Big Branch yearly.

In August, 1951, Jake had a freak accident. He was hauling tobacco on a wagon. The horses got into a yellow jacket's nest and got stung. In all the jumping around, they flipped the wagon. Jake jumped off, breaking his neck in the fall, which killed him.

This ended all the stories about Jake's mysteries.

Jake was my great uncle. He was a very special person and we all loved him very much. We were grateful for getting to know and love him. Dollie was my grandmother.

OUR HERO

Living in a farm house and taking care of the landlord's farm and livestock was a man, his wife, their children, two children of his sisters who had passed away. Then along came his daughter and her seven children after the death of his daughter's husband. By now some of his children had married and moved away. This was my new home and my family. When I was living there, there was a total of thirteen people. I must say, wall to wall people.

It was a major job, working for very little money, keeping up this family.

Grandpa did his work willingly, not grumbling. The landlord's farm was in good shape from his toil. He'd had no schooling. He could not read or write. He never knew if he was cheated from work on the farm or from the many hours he toiled just to keep a house for the family to live in. He trusted everyone.

Grandpa's only money was a share of the tobacco crop, and sometimes he was able to sell a few country hams. The weekly money that went for buying staples such as coffee, sugar, etc., came from selling a few dozen eggs.

He and his family grew vegetables, corn, and potatoes to preserve for winter use. When the cold days came he spent many days getting out wood for the landlord and for his family for heating and cooking.

Wiley Calwell, my grandpa,
and our hero.

Grandpa was happy when he completed a job and saw the benefits from it.

When Sundays came he walked four miles to and from church to see that the children were in church and that they had a chance to live God's way.

As the children worked with him and played he never fussed at them. He let them enjoy living.

He depended on the signs for planting his crops. He went by the moon and the sun to determine what the weather was to be and what time of day it was.

His work didn't end after the crops and wood were in for the winter. There was the livestock of the landlord's to be fed and taken care of. The cold weather days weren't passed sitting by the fire. He had work to do and willingly did it.

Never was there money in his pockets. What little money he had was taken care of by his wife and daughter. As the grandchildren grew older, one of them gave him a billfold with a few dollars in it. He was so happy with this, but he didn't carry it in his pocket for fear of losing it. Then one of them gave him a pocket watch. Again he was happy over this gift. He knew when both hands were at the top of the watch, it was twelve o'clock. He carried this occasionally on Sundays and showed it to his friends.

I must say my hero (my grandpa) was the greatest. We all loved him very much, as did everyone he came in contact with.

We were all grateful to be a part of his life and that he took us in, cared for us, and gave us a home. We learned to work, to love, to cope with life, and to live a Christian life.

In later years when I married, my husband and I built a home for Grandma, Mama, and him. This he deserved very much.

My grandpa has left this world to be in his home in Heaven and I'm sure he was well received as a hero angel.

He was absolutely the greatest hero ever.

I wish I could remember more of the stories Grandpa told me about some of the olden days when he was young. These are some of the ones I remember.

GRANDPA'S GRANDMA OWENS

"My Grandma Owens lived in Tennessee. She walked through the woods from Tennessee to where we lived at Fines Creek. She had visited with us a while and decided it was time to go home. So she started out one morning early about the time the roosters were crowing and figured she would be home before the roosters went to roost.

"After she didn't return home the folks set out through the woods to our house to see why she had not come home. They traveled for a while and someone saw a cloth hanging in a bush. They checked to see what the cloth was doing hanging away in the woods. To their surprise, the cloth was Grandma's kerchief and lying beside it was the handkerchief that she carried her little dab of money in. After looking around, they found her body! They had to go back into Tennessee and get the horses and sled to come back for Grandma's body. They had an idea who killed her, but they never could prove it."

GRANDPA'S DADDY, GREENBERRY CALDWELL

"Daddy was working at a saw mill at Fines Creek. He and some more of the men were walking home. Someone threw a rock. It hit Daddy on the shoulder and he fell over dead right there!"

GOD PROVIDED

On the 225-acre farm where my grandparents lived and where we moved when I was young, it seemed so many things grew wild.

In the early spring, we would watch complete fields of strawberries bloom. In a few weeks we picked many a gallon of strawberries for cobblers, jelly, and to can.

As the summer went along there were fields of blackberries, raspberries, dewberries, and in certain areas there were huckleberries. We also had currants and gooseberries.

After as many blackberries as my mother and grandmother needed to can, we picked and sold the extra for five cents a gallon. They were plentiful.

We were fortunate that the landlord had several apple trees and grapevines. These weren't wild, but they too were plentiful. In the summer horse apples and other tart apples were used for canning, drying, smoking, and making jelly. The old-timey sweet apple was good for baking and making preserves. In the fall of the year, there were huge trees of Sheepnose, Buff, and Bellflower apples that were gathered for winter use.

Even after the apples were gathered and until November, we could find the big apples nestled in the grass under the trees, which had protected them from freezing.

Fall was a busy time for us. As soon as the chestnut and chinquapins burrs started bursting open, we would gather them. Soon the ground would be covered with chestnuts. Each afternoon we picked up and the next afternoon there would be plenty more.

On the trail where we traveled to school, were several chestnut trees and there were many in the woods.

The chinquapins grew on bushes. There was one hill covered with them.

The chestnuts and chinquapins had to be gathered first, then the hazelnuts. The hazelnut grew on bushes, with hulls covering them. When the hulls became dark, you could lift the hazelnut out.

There were numerous hickory nut trees. We didn't have to worry about a burr. They had a thick hull and most of the time it fell off when they hit the ground.

The white and black walnuts were very hard to get the hulls off. When they first fell to the ground the hull was green. When the hull became brown, it was time to hull it. These hulls really stained our hands.

The hickory nuts, walnuts, and hazelnuts would keep a long time. They were stored away from the squirrels and to prevent freezing.

The persimmons and fox grapes were not good until the frost hit them. The fox grapes were excellent for jelly.

There were cressy greens and polk salad.

For meat there were squirrels, rabbits, and plenty of fish. It seems God provided for our needs.

We felt fortunate to live where we could go into the fields and woods to collect God's bounty. We were well blessed.

. . . and that's the way it was.
Louise

ABOUT THE AUTHOR

Louise Kinsland Nelson grew up in the Big Branch community in the 1920s and 1930s and attended the Big Branch one-room school. After graduation from high school in 1943, she and her husband, Floyd, owned and operated Nelson Radio and TV Service for thirty-five years.

Recently, Louise started writing for the *Waynesville Mountaineer* about the customs of early country living. After an outpouring of interest, she was encouraged to compile the stories into a book. She also had two writings in the *Reminisce* magazine, and other books are in progress.

Louise lives in Waynesville, N.C. and would welcome reader response.